A PEIPER'S TALE

for Peter Brotherton

A PEIPER'S TALE

Allan Peiper
with
Chris Sidwells

A PEIPER'S TALE

First published in 2005
Reprinted 2006
Reprinted 2007
by:

Mousehold Press   Sport & Publicity
Victoria Cottage   75 Fitzjohns Avenue
Constitution Opening   and   Hampstead
Norwich, NR3 4BD   London, NW3 6P
www.mousehold-press.co.uk   www.sport_publicity.co.uk

Cover design: El Tel Designs
Cover photograph: Phil O'Connor

ISBN: 978-1874739-39-5

Printed by Wrightsons, Earls Barton, Northants

Contents

Author's acknowledgements:
I would like to thank my mother and my father; Christina, my wife and partner of 20 years; my son, Zane, for being the light in my life; Eddy Planckaert for being there for me in so many different ways; my best friends Snake, Thomas Jackson, Simmo, Trowelly, Blacky and Phil, through whom friendship endures time; Paul and Denise for their constant support; and my boss, Marc Sergeant, for his faith in me, and for allowing a dream to come true.

I would also like to dedicate this book to Peter Brotherton, Olympic and World Silver medal-winner, for giving me back my legs, and for being my trainer, mentor, guru and father. He taught me to stand tall and be the best person I could, and he gave his patience and wisdom to me in every element of my life.

Publishers' Acknowledgements:
The publishers would like to thank the following people for their help, assistance and encouragement. In no particular order: Phil Liggett; Luke Evans; Jonathan Spruce (and his wife, Lizzy, who lets him go away to all the races in Belgium and France); Mick Clark; Chas Messenger (whose books he kindly gave us have been a fantastic help); Paul Sherwen; David Duffield; David Harmon; John Herety; Marilyn Bell; 'Rocky' Turner; Audrey; Patti; Anne Wooster; Steve Cummings and Bradley Wiggins (for helping Richard fall in love with cycle racing again). Special thanks for the production of *A Peiper's Tale* go to the authors, of course; Phil O'Connor; our cover designer, Terry 'El Tel' Batsford; and Sean Yates, whose foreword, and great friendship with Allan, inspired us from the start.
Thanks to you all.
Richard Allchin & Adrian Bell.

Photographic credits:
Colour section: Phil O'Connor;
B/w photos: author's collection

Publisher's Foreword

Of all the books I have published or been involved with, *A Peiper's Tale* is the one that is closest to my heart. For reasons I can't really explain I just knew that Allan had a great book to write. Call it luck or, if you are feeling generous, call it publisher's instinct.

It was through a good friend, Jonathan Spruce, and the fine writer and journalist, Chris Sidwells, that I first learned that Allan was very keen to write a book. In fact, talking to Allan recently, I realised that this had long been an ambition of his. However, at the time, I did not appreciate the depth of his passion, and his need, to write, share his life experiences, and open up his soul to the public. Maybe you could put this down to his egotism, which was a theme he continually dwelt upon throughout the first draft of the book. In reality, quite the opposite seemed to be true: here was a story written by a man of genuine modesty who seemed not to see that it was this very honesty and lack of ego that made his story so compelling, and his book so readable.

When I received the first drafts of the book I was immediately captivated by Allan's account of his childhood and his early days of racing. It was so different from the cycling books we had published, and I had read before. This was the story of his life, in all its aspects, and his candid style didn't leave a lot to the imagination. Further into the book, Allan related episodes of friendship, betrayal and jealousy, again without pulling any punches. His take on some of the biggest names in cycle racing during the last three decades was enthralling, and these are some of the most revealing in the book. Similarly, his opinions and shared experiences of doping are tackled with his natural frankness, and also with a refreshing optimism for the future. And here, as in the rest of the book, he never resorts to sensationalism. It was these qualities which convinced me that *A Peiper's Tale* should be published.

We at Sport & Publicity, and our co-publisher, Adrian Bell at Mousehold Press, are very proud to be associated with this fine book and would like to thank Allan and, of course, Chris Sidwells for their confidence in us. We hope the reader gets as much enjoyment and satisfaction from reading *A Peiper's Tale* as we have had in bringing it to publication. Enjoy.

Richard Allchin

Foreword

I was out running with Allan during the Tour of Romandie this year and, chatting away as we were, I reminded him about the time, long ago, when he sat with his bare feet in a bowl of hot water ten minutes before he was due to ride the prologue of the Tour of the Med. Laugh not – he won! He told me that that was the sort of stuff I should put in the foreword I was writing for his book.

We first got to know each other in 1983 when he joined the Peugeot team, which I was then a member of. Straight away he struck me as a man who knew exactly what he wanted, and that came as a real shock to me, because at that time I was just cruising along, not really knowing were I was going. His thoughts and ideas gave me a kick up the backside. Many of them I still have firmly embedded in my mind to this day – like the almond milk he got me drinking, and liking. 'Very good for you,' he said. Get a ton of almonds, drop them in boiling water for thirty seconds, peel them, grind them with a coffee grinder, tip into a blender, add a liberal dose of honey, top up with water and blend. Hey presto, almond milk. And absolutely delicious. Also about a million calories, which he forgot to tell me about; hence the Mister Blobby look-alike who used to go riding around in Peugeot kit.

But it wasn't just his concern that a racing cyclist needed to eat properly: I also got a taste of his discipline and dedication when I stayed with him in Belgium. His bike was always immaculately clean and his clothes perfectly folded. Training was at nine o'clock sharp, come rain or sunshine, and the tempo was always high. Once back we had a shower in a bathroom which had a little electric heater, and the water used to literally dribble out. There was no heating in the bedrooms, so we slept under a pile of about ten blankets, which just about crushed me.

I have so many fond memories of the times we have spent together, since those early years when we were trying to make our way as young pros. All great memories that I will cherish for the rest of my days. Like the mini-Olympics we set up when we were both staying at Surfers Paradise – he couldn't get over how good I was at tennis. And what was left of the tyres on that V8 Holden we rented. And what about the time I led him out for a time bonus sprint in the '84 Tour? He had the white jersey of the best young rider on his shoulders after coming third in the prologue and third in the first stage bunch finish – although how he managed that I still can't figure out. Anyway, he didn't come off my back wheel, like he should have done, but Jan Raas did. I turned round to Allan and snapped at him, 'That's the last bloody time I'm leading you out!' It was a bit cruel, and I don't know why he didn't hit me. The fact is, we complimented each other really well – the Little and Large Show. We lifted each other, especially when it came to time trials. And now, more than twenty years since we first met, we are back together on the continental circuit, trading wins and champagne like in this year's Giro.

In all the years I've known Allan I've never ceased to be amazed by the stories he tells of his upbringing. It was a tough one compared to mine, and it definitely shaped him in later life. Hearing those stories again made me – and I am certain many of you who will read his book – realise just how lucky we have been. What I am sure you will also get from *A Peiper's Tale* is a sense of the passion and feeling that Allan has for life, and for this sport of cycling.

Sean Yates

Winner of the Dulux Tour of New Zealand, 1981

INTRODUCTION

This book is not about my feats as a professional cyclist. I am not Eddy Merckx, and I am not Lance Armstrong. I did win some big races, I was a member of some of the best teams, and I helped some very good riders achieve their very best results; and, yes, I am proud of my career, proud to have been part of something I still love. But that is not the message of this book. What I have tried to do in it is show you what makes us, professional cyclists, tick, why we do what we do and what motivates us.

For example, although they are by no means the whole story of cycling there has been a lot of revelations over the last few years about drug use in the sport. And for the benefit of cyclist's health, and for the integrity of the sport, I applaud the efforts that have been made to control their use, even though those efforts have led to some painful publicity. Still, I feel that the cyclists have had no-one to stand up and tell how this situation came to be, tell why cyclists are tempted to take drugs, tell what pressures and what demands the sport entails.

But there is more. It is one thing to try and rid the sport of drugs, but another when an icon like Marco Pantani is hounded into an early death. It is also wrong when clean riders are branded with the same iron as the users. Innocent until proven guilty is surely the level-headed way. But there is a hysteria over drugs in sport. Why is that?

I tried to ride clean, most of the time. I know that sometimes riders beat me who had taken drugs, but I never felt they had stolen anything from me. All they had done was make a choice that I had been free to make, but didn't. Why should someone who has not been in the same situation get hysterical about that?

Nobody can bring Marco back. But guilty as he may have been, he was one of us, a brother who fought and died for what he loved, what we all love, cycling. He was nothing more, and certainly nothing less. Why was he persecuted?

Most of us are not innocent, but in this book I hope I will give you an understanding of the mechanisms working inside this sport we love. So, having read it, you may have a more understanding, more compassionate view of what we go through and what we do to get by. There are not just users and non-users. When is the line crossed? And once over, how do you get back? There is a whole grey area that is worth considering, one that just doesn't show up in a positive test.

Cycling is a very beautiful, but very vulnerable sport. We talk and act tough, but there are many romantics out there riding bikes in the professional peloton. I cried many times when I read Lance Armstrong's book. Not because it was sad, but because it resonated with so many parts of my own life. In it I saw my anger and my love of cycling, but above all it spoke to me of the humanity and dignity in Lance's suffering.

I had raced with Lance in my final year as a pro. It was my last race, the Tour of Ireland. He was a brand-new pro with Motorola, having been an amateur up to the Olympics earlier in 1992. I was going out the back and he was going off the front, and I thought; who is this kid?

By the next year's Tour de France, he had won a stage and stopped after ten days, and I was working for the British and Australian TV on the race, doing commentary. The night before the final stage that is held on the Champs Élysées in Paris I had dinner with the TV team, but decided to go back to my room and get some sleep when the rest of them suggested moving on to a night-club at about midnight.

Outside in the street, trying to get a taxi, I heard a voice call out. It was Lance, a girl on each arm and a beer in each hand. He wanted me to go for a drink with him. I was just out of cycling, doing a job that was taking all I'd got, and I wasn't very good at it. At home my wife was calling my bluff with 'Pull your socks up, or it's all over'. It wasn't my best moment; I felt sorry for myself and vulnerable. I tried to explain; I told Lance I was going back to my hotel, and why. 'Oh, you're a fucking pussy Peiper,' he yelled. There were people all around us. He was already the man, and I was crushed.

I bore him a grudge after that, and I even swore that I wouldn't read his book. Then one day I was staying with my good friend Blacky up on the Gold Coast in Queensland, and there was a copy of Lance's book in the lounge and in my bedroom. I thought to myself, 'Well this is it, Al.' I read it and like many of you I was completely taken by this young man, his struggle and his love for cycling. I even felt he said sorry to me.

We are a mixed-up bunch, us cyclists, not balanced like most people. We run on our egos, and hide our frustrations and impressions of life in our actions. A lot of our life is lived in denial, then we stop racing and the rooster comes home. It's then that we get the bill.

This book is about the inside of a cyclist, what he feels and what his world looks like from the saddle. Read about me only as a reference, as a base to the rest of the story.

With Grandfather 'Bill' Peiper, State Cycling Champion in 1935

1

The Peipers

This book is about cycling, but to know how I tick and to understand why I did the things I did in my life you need to know something about my background. Everybody has a story to tell, some better, some worse; but it's all relative. It's the impressions of our life, formed by experiences that create our personalities. We all have different experiences and we act differently because of the impressions that those experiences leave.

For example, what drives cyclists to suffer in the Tour de France for 21 days? I believe it is the sum total of our experiences and the impressions they leave; cycling is just the vehicle we use to express ourselves, to vent our frustrations, to feel good about ourselves and to be accepted. I want to share my experiences with you because it will help you to know where I come from and what created a burning desire to excel, and push myself to the limit to succeed.

When I was ten years old I lived in a small town called Bannockburn in Victoria, Australia. I rode my bike everywhere, with my faithful old dog Scrooge running alongside me. I'd rescued Scrooge from a rubbish pit near to another town we'd lived in a few years earlier. He was the ugliest dog you have ever seen, but he could run like the wind and used to catch rabbits and eat them in the thorn bushes, while I had to wait for him.

Scrooge and I used to explore all the creeks and rivers in the area, staying out all day and taking lunch with us. Well, I took mine; Scrooge had to catch his. On one particular day we hiked along this river, me pretending to be the first white person ever to enter the area. I lived like that then, inside my head, doing things on my own. I liked it that way.

It was evening by the time we headed home, and as we walked across a paddock, through long grass with the autumn wind blowing in my face, I could feel my legs getting tired, but I still had a long climb on my bike up onto the plateau before I got home.

You must have had those moments in your life, whether they are a thought, an experience or a feeling. They are like signposts, moments that stay with you forever and seem to colour the rest of your life. This was one of them. It came to me then, the thought – keep going Allan, this will make you fit and strong. I was ten and knew nothing of what was to come in my life, knew nothing of how that thought would shape my life, and how it would test me physically and mentally to the limits of my existence.

I was born Allan Bruce Peiper in Alexandria, which is also in Victoria. My mother, Esther, had grown up there, but my father, Bruce, was from Yea, about 20 miles away. My grandfather on my mother's side was a truck driver, who owned his own fleet of trucks, but who crashed into a ravine and broke his neck. He recovered, but he lost his business in the process. My other grandfather was a sheep-shearer; possibly one of the best in Australia, having shorn well over 100,000 sheep in his career. He was also a Victorian State junior cycling champion in the 1930s.

As you can see, I came from hard stock, people who worked hard and struggled to get ahead. Both my grandfathers were fending for themselves from a very early age, and up until she was six years old my mother lived in what they call in Australia a 'bark humpy', a shack built up against a tree trunk and covered with bark.

My father worked in a bank and my mother was a nurse, and from the day I was born we were always on the move. My father was good at his job, receiving promotion after promotion, becoming a branch manager by the time he was 30, but it meant that, on average, we moved to a new town every six months.

Even when I was young my parents had an up-and-down relationship, like so many of us do. My father drank, and he and my mother would argue. Sometimes she left him, taking me and my sister with her, but then halfway to the city she would stop the car, look over at me in the dark and say; 'Shall we go home to daddy?'

My younger sister would be asleep in the back and it would be left to me, the big five year old, to decide. 'Yes Mum let's go home,' I would say, and she'd turn the car around and drive back. She loved him and didn't have the courage to leave him. When we got back it would be a warm welcome for a few days, and then things would slip back again.

My mother often used to work away from home and take my sister with her. Then my father's drinking was a problem for me. I would go to school during the day, but when I got home the house was empty, no lights on, and I would have to fend for myself, knowing that I was alone until Dad came home. My mother only went for a few weeks, but those times used to seem like months to me.

One time I woke up in the dark and thought I saw somebody come into my room and walk over to my bed. I hid under the blankets, petrified. Finally I came out and went through the house, calling for my father, but there was no answer. I ran out the back door, down the garden, through a hole in the fence and across the highway. I ran into the pub, but the pub was just closing – it was ten at night. The barman took me to the police station, and I stayed there until they found my father.

When we moved to Bannockburn in 1970 things got worse with my father's drinking. His mother had a stroke, caused by a tumour on her brain. She was back in Yea, waiting her time to go, but my father had just taken promotion in Bannockburn, 200 kilometres away. And now from the drinking came violence, which for me would last the next six years, until I finally left home.

I was a child who was always playing outside. I had rabbit traps out in the bush, and I hunted with a ferret. It was nothing for me to climb out of my bedroom window at 6 am to go and check on my traps before I went to school. I fished night and day, too.

My other joy was a small transistor radio. I went to bed each night and lay there listening to the sounds of the Doors and Rod Stewart, the radio on my pillow and my ear pressed close to it, so that no one else, especially my dad, could hear.

When I was ten I began to have trouble at school. The head teacher disliked me intensely. If anything went wrong, it would be me who did it, whether it was or not. Then it was the strap across my legs.

Not that I was a saint. My first girlfriend went to that school in Bannockburn; her name was Tracey and she sat at the desk in front of me. One day I tied her pig tails to the back of her chair, but the teacher saw me do it, and hit me so hard on my shoulder with his fist that I landed on the other side of my desk. That teacher said I would end up in jail, but only a few years later it was he who ended up there, convicted of child molesting.

If anything happened in the town, like a haystack being burned down or a house broken into, the police would come to our place. My dad hated that, as he had some standing in the town, being the bank manager. Every time they came I was grounded. But after a while the town policeman became my friend. He was a nice guy and he respected me and used to take me to the football in Geelong every Saturday. Maybe he thought that it was his duty to help the town's delinquent.

At school I was the best at sports, any sports: football, cricket or athletics. When I was 11, I played with the town's under-15 boys football team. They needed a full 18-man team, but there was so few of them that I got picked every week. Not that they were any good, every week we got beaten.

One time some of the parents driving the team to a match got lost, so we had to play with 10 men until half time, when the rest arrived. We'd been holding the score even until then, but with a full team we lost by so much that you don't need to know.

I begged my parents for a bike every Christmas from when I was six, and always got an intellectual present, like a camera. I could have thrown it against the wall; I wanted a bike. I had learned to ride on the football field in Maffra, another place we lived in, on a friend's bike, and the feeling of freedom I got from riding it was one I couldn't let go of.

Finally, on my eleventh birthday I got my first bike. Not a chopper, like all the kids got then; not me. I got an old second hand racing bike with a fixed wheel. I didn't know about the fixed wheel until I went round my first corner with my enthusiasm flying as high as a kite, and grounded the pedal … Touchdown! My first gravel rash.

I loved that old wreck, but when my sister got her bike the next year it was open season. It was smaller and had a wheel brake. I could go out and do jumps on it, and I raced a few of my mates in time trials around our block. Even on my sister's bike I could wipe the floor with them.

My sister, Jennifer, who is three years younger than me, was a beautiful child with long blond hair. We missed each other a lot when she went away from time to time with my mother. From that night when I went running through the streets looking for my father I had been afraid of the dark, and if I woke up scared in the night I knew I could always climb into bed with Jen and I would be safe.

She loved me and looked up to me as well. Once we had an athletics carnival with a few different schools, and I cleaned up in all the events. Jennifer came over to show me the certificate she had received for a third prize. I was already self-centered by then, and didn't pay Jen the attention she deserved. I remember her dejected look, but I didn't pick up on it. I have always regretted that moment. I can still feel her disappointment and pain. Later, that was another signpost for me. It became important for me to acknowledge other people's efforts in life.

With Jennifer, my sister – 1965

Our lives are a tangle of impressions gained from experiences, which superimpose on top of each other. We build up this hard-drive of memories that motivate our thoughts, actions and feelings. Sometimes I see it as spider's web. The spider starts in the middle and works its way outwards, forming ring after ring, each one joined by short strand lines, which are the impressions left by our experiences. Over time the web gets bigger and there is no unthreading it back to the centre. We are as we are, a product of our experiences.

As time went by my father's bouts of violence grew, he started hitting my mother; one time he even hit her with a frying pan. It pained me to see her hurt, and to see her tired out by working to pay the bills, while he went through all his money himself.

Then one night there was a dance in town, a family dance with waltzes and the foxtrot. It didn't happen very often, and I asked my mum if I could go. Dad would be at the pub giving his arm some exercise, so she said that it would be ok until ten.

I went, but after a while one of the guys on the door came into the hall and said my mum was out front, and that I had to go. I went out getting ready to plead my case for staying, but saw she had been crying and had a swelling on her face. When we got home my father went crazy, he took the lead from the water-heater and took into me with it. He just kept hitting and hitting me with it. It was then that the hate began, the rage inside was unleashed and a driving will to succeed was born.

At about the time that this happened we were driving from Bannockburn to Yea twice a week to see my grandmother, Florence, in hospital. It was a difficult time for me; my father's mother was everything for me that love could be. I used to go to her place on holidays, and she baked me chocolate sponge cake with cream in the middle and icing on top, or jam roly-poly cake. But when we went to the hospital Jennifer and I weren't allowed to go in and see her. Maybe it was because my grandfather, who was so strict, found us children intolerable. We weren't allowed to walk on the grass at his house, or enter the lounge room. On holidays I used to have to sleep out on the balcony.

One night near the end, during visiting hour, my mother came out of the hospital and got me. Nan had asked for me. She had not been speaking for some time, but that night she had asked for me. I went to her bed, and she took my hand with the one hand she could still use and said; 'I love you Allan.' I never saw her again, but I can still hear her voice, if I listen very hard.

Grandmother Florence (left), Great Granny Cochrane(centre), Auntie Nancy, Dad's sister (right). The baby is Nancy's son, Christopher, who also raced bikes.

2

Diggy, Clicker and Tambo

My father had asked for a transfer to Yea so he could be close to his mother, but by the time he was told we could move, Nan had died and been buried. Moving had become a way of life for me, packing everything into tea chests, and then the removers would come and load our stuff, taking it to the next destination.

In all, I went to fourteen schools. Leaving your friends, your school, your house, time after time was getting harder for me. Each place we went to I was the new kid on the block, the whole school looking at me, adding to my persecution complex. I was sure they were laughing at me or talking about me.

In Bannockburn I left Tracy behind. I was too young for her to be a real girlfriend, but our families were close. She wore glasses, had long brown hair and was the smartest girl in the school. I was a rough-and-tumble kid, but our differences held us together. When we went to school in Geelong, she went on a different bus to a different school, and I missed her. I would end up missing a lot of people in my life. I was a gypsy from birth, always moving.

When we arrived in Yea, I loved it from the word go. I made new friends, Diggy, Clicker and Tambo, and did we get up to some shit together. Like all small Australian towns, all there was to do was drink, and you had to start early. Saturday nights I would scale down the drain-pipe from the second floor of the bank, and meet the guys at the back of the middle pub.

We'd start off with six cans of Fosters each, under the second bridge, and would end up riding our bikes home nearly paralysed drunk. Diggy's father ran the town newspaper, and Diggy had a rack on the front of his bike for delivering the papers. One Saturday night we had loaded up at the pub and were heading down to the river, to sit under the second bridge, when in the dark on the gravel road somebody said, 'Right,' and Diggy went left. Bikes, cans and kids crashed all over the road. We laughed until we cried, and then drank our beer. The joke lasted until my mother saw the footprints on the window sill I'd made when I came off the drain-pipe.

There was a boy at my school called Murray Collins, who raced with the under-16s in the Alexandra Cycling Club. I was interested in all sports but knew nothing about cycling. It was Murray who told me all about it, about track racing and road. He was an experienced 15 year old; I was coming up to 13. He told me all about the Tour de France and showed me magazines like *Miroir du Cyclisme* from France and *Cycling Weekly* from England. He talked of going to race in France, but I brushed this off, worldly, know-all teenager that I was trying to be.

There was an old racing frame in our garage at home, and Murray came round to have a look at it. He was going to Melbourne the next week with his father, and said he would bring me back everything I needed to get started. My mother, who supported me in everything I did, gave me the money for the parts, and enough for a pair of shoes for racing, shorts and a racing jersey.

When he got back, Murray put the bike together and we went on a few rides for me to get used to it. The bike had a fixed wheel because it was the track season. There were no traffic lights where we lived for 100 kilometres and no traffic to worry about, except for the odd cattle truck.

My first race was in Alexandra, on a dirt track around a football field. I had three races in the under-14 category; – two handicaps and a scratch race – and I won them all. It was so easy to win; I was sold.

In all the other sports I did, I had to rely on other people to win, like in football, basketball and cricket. Even in badminton and tennis you needed to play doubles, often to my disgust. That was one trait I got from my father's family, being as hard as nails on everyone around me. His family came from Germany. That says it all really, doesn't it?

Murray and I had gone over to Alexandra in the car with our parents, but decided to ride the twenty miles home. We had to walk up Eglington cutting, just outside Alexandra, because my 72-inch gear was too big for the climb. On the way back Murray kept telling me how this 'winning' thing I'd just done wouldn't happen all the time, and I needed to realise it would get harder. He didn't know how much harder!

During the ride Murray's bike kept making noises, coming from what he called the 'centre bracket'. We had one more climb before we arrived in Yea, and the noises from Murray's bike were getting louder. Murray's home life was a bit like mine. His dad had been a Golden Gloves boxing champion and had gotten a bit punchy, so much so that he sometimes used his wife as a sparring partner. So Murray had a temper. We were climbing Cotton's Pinch and were getting close to the top when Murray dismounted, lifted up his bike, went into a discus spin and with a guttural scream heaved his bike over the edge in disgust.

My family life was spinning out of control by this time. My mother had been into hospital for a few operations. She was tired from years of night duty and double shifts to keep the house going. Added to that, and for me the most important factor, was her emotional state after years of abuse. I think negative emotions are much more poisonous to your health than anything physical, within reason. Dad was drunk every day, but he was proud of me and would take my trophies into the bank to show everybody. It didn't help, I hated him doing that. He promised me once that if I trained he would clean my bike, but he never cleaned it once.

Many nights I would lay in bed listening to the build up of emotions between my parents, shaking with fear as I lay there, knowing what was coming. The argument would reach a crescendo and my mother would scream. I would be out of bed and in there, just in time to see him land a punch in her face. Blind rage would take me over, and I would drag his stinking carcass of a body off her and lay into him with my fists. Eventually Mum would get in between us and get us apart. I would be sent back to bed and they would make up. I would get the blame. As neurotic as it sounds, it's the truth. Throw another log on the fire of rage.

Then came another signpost. I had been in the living room watching television, when I heard my mother scream and ran to protect her. They were in the kitchen, and he was hitting her when

I got there. Like so many times before I went into a blind rage. This time, though, it was different. I hit him and he went down, smashing his head against the kitchen bench, which opened a big gash on his forehead.

He hit the ground. I had Dutch clogs on my feet and I started kicking him with only one thought in my mind; to kill him, kill him, kill him! It just took me over and I had no control, but at the same time I saw clearly through all the insanity that that was the only way we could get out of this hell of a life. To kill him.

My mother was screaming at me to stop. I could hear her back there somewhere. She fell on him, to protect him. She loved him so much that nothing could break her love. Suddenly I was frightened at what had become of me, and unconsciously I knew that I could never let that animal out again. The anger had to stay inside. I loved my dad, but there was nothing good about the life we had.

That incident happened in 1975, and throughout the rest of the year life took its own course. A lot of the boys I raced with had birthdays and went into the next age-group category.

In the summer of 1975/76 I won two Australian track championships, the sprint and the 5-kilometre scratch race. The championships were in Melbourne and my mother went with me, even though I didn't like anybody close to me watch me race in those days.

I turned junior in the April of 1976 and took more time off school to train. Most of the teachers were tolerant and supportive towards me. If we went on a school camp they always let me take my bike so I could train. In fact I was held in near idol status at school. I was aloof and angry and needed no one, but the biggest thing was that I was successful and that made me accepted.

On Wednesdays we had sport in the afternoon, and I had a pass from school to train, but before that, on Wednesday mornings we had wood-work. Now I'm not a handy man, even as a child the sight of a Meccano set would make me feel sick. If I went to school on Wednesday morning all I got was a four hour planing project, the teacher would give me a block of wood and tell me to plane it flat, an impossible and unending job. So what I did was go to school, get my name checked off the register and go home again to go riding.

14

I was good at mathematics, and especially good at writing. If we had to do a review of a book, I could write a thousand words just from what was on the front sleeve and hearsay from the other kids. It was too easy.

I won a lot of road races during that Australian winter as a sixteen year old junior. It was Olympic year, and two of the Australian squad, five-times National Champion Remo Sansonnetti and his twin brother Sal, were in the Victorian team, but I didn't get a good start with those two.

I had joined the squad the previous year as a schoolboy, and went with the team to the National Road Championships in Hobart, Tasmania. I was getting on the truck one night to go to dinner and Remo yelled out in front of everyone that I was 'a wanker'. I was just 15 and learning about my sexuality, and Remo's remark hurt me. I swore that I would make him pay for it one day.

My chance came in a race shortly after the Olympics. It was in a town called Horsham, in which I had lived for a short while some years before. I went to the race with my new friend Brian Gillin, in his car. Brian was 21 and I looked up to him. He was a tough cookie with tattoos.

The juniors raced with the amateurs in those days, and in the 110-kilometre main race six of us were together at the finish – four Olympians, Brian and myself. I remember thinking 400 metres out that even if I was last in the sprint I would still be sixth. Somehow I just let that sprint unfold and followed the wheel in front of me. I was in the flow. I hit the wind 100 metres out. Remo was leading, but inch by inch I pulled him back, beating him by a tyre on the line. It was a sweet revenge.

It was about that time that I first remember guys talking about feeling pain in their legs when they were racing or training. I never knew what they were talking about, because it never happened to me. Not until a few years later, when I got sick in Belgium, did I learn about suffering and going through the pain barrier, because until then I never felt it. The greatest racer of all time, Eddy Merckx, says that until 1969, when he injured his back during a crash at a track meeting in Blois, France, he never felt his legs. After the crash he suffered like the rest, even though he won hundreds of races.

I once read an article about Michael Jordan, the basketball player with the Chicago Bulls. He said that once, in an NBA final with only a handful of seconds remaining and the Bulls trailing by one point, he scored the winning goal. But he said that in the moment he scored it, while he was in mid-air, he saw the whole picture. Suddenly he left our linear world, a world proscribed by normal human senses, and saw the thoughts of the defenders, and the outcome of the game.

If you have ever done top sport maybe you have entered that zone, or one like it. One where you were just in the flow, and it all happened without you making it happen. It was like that often for me before I got ill, never after, and it is sport's greatest secret. If you could tap that, turn it on whenever you needed it, there would be no need for chemical enhancers.

Meanwhile back home, in September 1976, we had another heartbreaking brawl, but this time my mother packed us up and we all left my father. My mother had nursed an old man in the hospital she worked at. They had become friends and she turned to him for a place to stay while she sorted things out.

Then one day, as I was coming back to the old man's place from school, she was standing at the gate waiting for me. She told me that she was going back to my father. I felt my chest tighten, my legs go weak and my heart cry out in pain. I told her that if she went back then it would be without me. To my amazement she said, 'OK'. I was 16 years old; the feeling of rejection was almost unbearable. It broke my heart to give her that ultimatum. But for once, after every fight they had and me coming to her aid every time, I wanted her to choose me. When she didn't, it hurt me more than I can say.

My more immediate need was where was I going to live. Frank Cunningham, the father of a friend of mine, and who had a heart as big as anyone I have ever known, offered me a bed in his home, and for that I am grateful to this day, but it couldn't be a permanent solution.

Also, from that day, I had to start paying my way in the world. Frank would have helped me out, I know, but I was too proud to ask. The first thing I did was tell my teachers that I was leaving school. Many of them were upset, they could see my potential and some even offered to give me lessons after they'd finished their day at work, so I could keep going for my exams, which were only weeks away.

Now I wish that I had taken their help, but I couldn't be helped in those days. I was stubbornly independent. The last few years have made me realise that qualifications would have helped me now. If you are a pro cyclist you finish your career in your mid-thirties, when people outside of sport have established themselves and are at their most dynamic. There we are, ravaged by years of training, racing and suffering; most of our physical and a lot of our mental reserves gone, and then comes another set of battle conditions – the real world. Everything there depends on qualifications, and until then we've done all our talking with our legs. It's a hard transition, and those that say it isn't either earned enough money, or are very lucky, very together people.

I finished school at the end of year eleven, three weeks before the exams. My mother wanted me to be a doctor, and maybe that is what I'd have chosen for myself, but now I had another focus – my bike, although at best it was only an avenue through which I could express my frustrations.

School was over and I had to build another life. All I'd got was cycling. I got a job in a factory that spray painted office furniture, but I hated it. My wages were 60 dollars a week, and I gave ten to Frank for my board. The rest I saved because my mate, Brian, was going to Belgium to race in the April of 1977, and I'd asked him if I could go with him. It would be my escape.

I was still 16 years old and my mother had to sign some papers giving me permission to leave the country. I phoned her about it and we met at a set of traffic lights on the highway at Southland shopping centre. It was a very emotional meeting and my mother gave me 300 dollars to take with me. It was the difference I needed for my air fare. I'd saved the rest, 25 times 50 dollars a week from my wages.

An air traffic controllers' strike kept us on the ground for two weeks, but eventually the day came. As I sat in my window seat before take-off, I could see my mother standing on the viewing deck. I wanted it to be different, I wanted to climb out of the plane and take her in my arms. But it wasn't different; it was like this. I could see her crying; her baby was leaving. She was so small at that moment, a shell of a person ravaged by love and hate.

My mother

3

Jan 'The Papers'

Thirty years ago intercontinental travel was still a dream for most people. Flying from Australia to Europe was an epic 25-hour journey, with at least three stops to re-fuel along the way, but I was on my way. I couldn't believe it, and I certainly had no idea of what I was getting into. I'd heard all the stories about the Australian riders who'd gone to Europe before me – Sir Hubert Opperman, Russell Mockridge, Alf Strom, Reg Arnold, Ron Baensch, Danny Clarke, the Allan brothers, Don and David and Peter De Longville. It was De Longville, a mate of my travelling companion Brian, who had given us our contact in the place we were eventually aiming for: Ghent in Belgium.

There were many more Aussies who went to Europe, too. But all came back with stories that were enough to scare you half to death. Stories of poverty, cold and hunger were common, so were tales of the typical 'tough Aussie battler' fighting overwhelming odds to get one over the locals. And then there were the locals. I'd read about them in Murray Collins' cycling magazines. Eddy Merckx, Francesco Moser, Roger de Vlaeminck and my own hero, Freddy Maertens. Awesome men. I couldn't wait.

Before we got to Ghent we had to land in London. The experiences were coming thick and fast. I just had to travel on a big red bus, and it had to be upstairs, but it was a freezing cold, grey London day. Still, I got my ride and we lugged our bikes up and down the stairs, along with a tool bag, a suitcase and another bag, each.

We loaded all our stuff on and off buses and trains. It was Hell, but finally we made Dover and the overnight ferry to Ostend. I was so tired after nearly 48 hours of travelling, and my arms ached with all I was carrying. After midnight we boarded the train in Ostend for Ghent, took a taxi to the Hotel den Ijzer in the Vlaanderenstraat, and there on the third floor I slept like a rose, blissfully unaware of the new life awaiting me next morning.

Our only connection in Ghent was the address of an old lady, Rosa De Snerck. Her husband owned the Plume Vainqueur bike shop, and she had helped many foreign bike riders find accommodation in the city. One of her favourites had been Brian's mate, Peter De Longville, who we called 'Smelly'.

We left our bags behind in the hotel and went in search of Rosa's house. I felt safe with Brian; we were together and he was like a big brother. But when we got to Rosa's, she told us that she had no room. She asked us to return next day and in the meantime she would try and find us somewhere else to stay.

That night was spent in a hostel in Ghent. Well, I say hostel, but it was more like a half way house. Brian had to sleep in another room and there were about ten men in my room. Dirty, smelly, drunk men, who snored and made all manner of other noises. I was frightened – these were very new circumstances for me. I lay there with my arms strung through the handles of all my bags, in case someone tried to rob me. It was a long way from the comfort of my mother. I was on my own, but I knew there was no way back. In the morning we went back to Rosa's, and she had found us a house 50 metres up the hill in St Kwintensberg. It was an old butcher's shop and there were about ten riders and some students already living in the building.

The only room available was the shop space itself. Jan, the owner, put some multiplex over the window, and put another piece at 90 degrees from the door to form a hallway into the house. That gave us some privacy, but we still had no door to close behind us. Jan also put in a bunk and Rosa gave us some sheets, blankets, a pillow each and some cooking utensils. I took the top bunk because I thought it would be the safest.

The owner of the building was quite a scary character. Jan 'The Papers' we called him, because he collected newspapers to sell for re-cycling. He slept in the room next to ours, and you had to go through it to get to the communal kitchen and toilet, but it wasn't an easy task. Jan's room was piled high with newspapers, and there was a sort of track that wound through the room between the stacks.

The first night we slept there was the only time I got up to go to the toilet. Staggering through Jan's pitch black room I nearly stepped on his sleeping body. It scared me to death and after that I just went outside and urinated in the gutter if I needed to.

But the rumour was that Jan was rich and owned many houses; he just lived like a hermit, on the edge of society. He found his food in the dustbins at the back of supermarkets, and I would often see him eating rotten fruit in the kitchen. Once I saw him washing at the kitchen sink. He was washing his long, matted hair and upper body with a cloth and the dirt was running down his back into his pants. One time the toilet was blocked, but people had still used it. It was full of faeces and paper, but Jan fixed it. He just rolled up his sleeve, reached into the bowl through the whole unspeakable mess, shoulder deep, and removed the blockage with his bare hand.

My first training ride in Belgium was an eye-opener. We left with the other guys from the house at 9 am, and went to pick up some others who lived outside Ghent. Once we got to their place we sat around for an hour while they ate toast, then we rode 40 kilometres at 25 kilometres an hour. I was frozen stiff from riding so slow. It was the last time I ever rode with them.

Next day I was out at 8 am and rode for four hours on my own. I was 17, but I knew about discipline. I did the same every day after that. Routine is everything to me, and I needed to create a routine that gave me some semblance of normality in this world of change and new experiences I'd landed in.

My next problem, though, was getting a licence to race in Belgium. A first-year junior in Belgium, a foreigner as young as I was and wanting to race in Belgium, was unprecedented in those days. There was a race nearly every day in Flanders, but I couldn't get in them. I was getting desperate, I had enough money to last one month. I had to race soon to win some more.

Brian was racing by now with the amateurs. He had met a guy called Staf Boone at one of his races. Staf loved foreign riders and would do anything to help, but I had heard bad things about him to do with drugs, so I steered clear. However, it was Staf who came to my rescue. He heard of my plight and took me to see a high-ranking cycling official who lived in the Ghent area. Next day I had my licence, and I had started a friendship with Staf and his family that lasts to this day.

Still, it was a tough start. My first race was in Zottegem. I got in the break, but I had been riding every day for a month on one set of tyres and they were nearly worn through. I punctured on the last lap and only got home because another Australian, David Brotherton, the son of British Olympic rider Peter Brotherton, lent me a tyre. I was at the bottom of the barrel, but Staf Boone was there to fish me out again. That night he came round to the house with two new tyres. I was back in business.

Next day I rode 20 kilometres to a race at Gavere, but wasn't allowed to start as it was a team race, and I had no team. Never mind, ten kilometres further on there was a race at Eine. I took off fast to make the start. I needed the money. I had no food, no tyres. It had to happen today.

I made the start, just, all wound up and nervous, and then I saw him. I'd heard about him; he was already a legend – three times a Belgian champion in four years of racing, and winner of 50 races a year – Eddy Planckaert. Younger brother of Tour de France Green Jersey winner, Willy, and the Tour of Flanders winner, Walter, the latest member of a Flanders dynasty.

He was wearing his black, yellow and red national champion's jersey, and he was so brown, so tanned, he was almost black. When you are racing you can see when a guy is on form; it is like you can see, almost feel, their energy. It shines just below the surface of their skin. The class was dripping off Eddy. I had never seen a bike rider like him.

After two laps of the race Eddy attacked and got a 100-metres lead. I attacked, got away from the bunch, caught him and went straight past. To this day he says he never saw anybody who could ride as fast as I did when I went past him, and it took all he had to catch me up.

We started to share the lead, but as the race developed I found out why Eddy had such a fearsome reputation. There were sprints for cash prizes called primes every lap, but try as I might I couldn't out-sprint Eddy.

As we went into the last lap I knew I would lose if it came to a sprint. So long before the finish I attacked and kept on attacking.

Nothing for nothing, if he was going to win he would have to earn it. The rage was burning inside me. I needed the money, but he hadn't let me win one sprint.

Still, I couldn't shake him off. I led out the sprint, but he was so fast he won by lengths. He says that as we crossed the line I spat at him. I don't remember that, but I can imagine that in the anger of losing I could have spat in his direction. Staf Boone used to call me 'de nijdig baasje'. It sort of means the 'angry kid'. He was right, too, and some.

However, back in Ghent I did find a brotherhood with the guys around me. There were 15 of us in Jan's house at one time, all bike riders from five English speaking nations. One of them was Mike Tanks, an English kid who was a year older than me.

Mike was a track rider who lived by the seat of his pants. He had grown up in central London, tough as nails; rude, brash, outspoken and he dared nothing. He was all the things I wasn't, but for some reason we clicked, and as Brian had made his own friends through racing with the amateurs, an older category than I was in, Tanks was my new buddy.

Rumour has it that the six-day rider, Gary Wiggins, the father of 2004 Olympic Gold Medallist Bradley, had rubbed Tanks up the wrong way when they were racing on a track in London one day. That night Tanks found an open window at the track and climbed through to where Wiggins kept his bike. He had a hacksaw with him and neatly sawed through the bike's top-tube, just far enough that it didn't go right through, but could snap when Wiggins was in full flight. Now, Gary Wiggins was a man to be scared of, at least I was, but not Tanks.

Tanks used to have this huge great coat, which he wore in the mornings to keep warm, because there was no heating. Tanks would wake up, don the great coat and cross the street to the local store. The owner lived at the back of the shop, but before he could make it down the hallway Tanks would have the many pockets inside that coat filled with Mars bars, biscuits, or whatever he could get his hands on. Every day he bought just one egg, but every day the owner got faster at coming down the hallway, and soon Tanks didn't have time to steal anything.

Our friendship didn't extend to training together. Mike came with me once, but soon got the message. We did ride to races together, though. No one had a car, so we went everywhere by bike. At one race it was announced over the speakers that I'd won a supporter's prime. Before the race I was unwell; I hadn't been eating because I'd no money. This guy at the race said I needed a steak to build me up, it must have been him who donated the money.

I didn't get the steak. My bike came first, and I spent the money on that. I had some potatoes at home and riding home with Tanks we spotted what we thought was spinach growing in a field. We got off and filled my back pack with the green leaves, got home, boiled them up with the potatoes and covered the whole lot in ketchup. It was only later that we found out that what we'd been eating wasn't spinach, but the tops of sugar beet that the farmers used to give their animals in winter.

It was cold in the house, and I was lonely and frightened when I was there on my own. Brian would often be away racing, and get back late at night. There was no door on our room and the door to the street was never locked. I would lay in my bunk from nine o'clock, which was my bed time, waiting for Brian to come home. As soon as he came in I'd go to sleep.

The place where we lived was terrible. In the mornings Jan the Papers used to stoke up the boiler by burning old paper that was too dirty to re-cycle and whatever else he could find. It really was a filthy, rat-infested house. There was one shower, but the hot water was limited to those who sprinted back first from training. The last guys always got freezing water.

I missed my mother desperately and constantly wrote letters home to her. I can remember standing at the red letter-box on the corner with a letter in my hand, reluctant to let go, wishing I could go back with it. But what would I be going back to? Nothing. I couldn't go back.

It was then that I learned how to deal with homesickness. If I allowed my mind to wander, or any weakness to creep in, the homesickness would be back. I went through an agony I still find hard to put into words. The only thing to do was what the Dutch rider, Henk Lubberding, used to say about suffering in races years later when I knew him in the Panasonic team: 'Just put your mind on zero,' he used to say.

At least there were plenty of races to take my mind off thoughts of home. The only problem was that in every race I rode, Eddy Planckaert was there. He lived about 20 kilometres from Ghent and there were a lot of races in his area. Not that many juniors used to ride them. It was Eddy's turf, and they knew they couldn't win.

For me, though, that wasn't important. The difference between first and second place was only about 100 francs, about one pound. Eddy and I always ended up off the front together, and Eddy would always win. Then there came a time when we began to share the lap prizes. Eddy had realized he would win but it was better to be on good terms with me. I was his perfect helper. Instead of everyone waiting for him to make a move, now he had a strong rider to attack, get away and he would jump across to me. We were a class above the rest, perfect pro juniors, and our reputation began to spread across the land.

Eddy was already a star. Hundreds of supporters followed him, even if there were only twenty riders in a race, and he was receiving £100 start money in every race he rode. That was a lot of money in 1977, especially for a young amateur!

We became friends, prickly friends on my part, but genuine friends. After a wet race in Vosselaar, a village near to his home Eddy offered to drive me home to Ghent, but first we had to go to his house. It was grey and drizzling outside as we entered the half-dark kitchen. Inside, at the table sat Eddy's mother playing cards with his older brothers, Willy and Walter. I was in awe at being in such godly company. These men had reputations that made them talked about across Flanders with reverence by fans and riders alike. I stood in stunned silence at their presence, and they nodded hello, turning back to their game. English hadn't crossed the Channel yet.

When Eddy got to my place in Ghent, he couldn't believe the squalid conditions I was living in. He took pity on me there and then, I could see it. My good friend Scott Sunderland said to me recently that we all need a guardian angel to guide us at times. I had found one of mine. Someone who would look over me. Someone who would guide me. Someone who would care about what happened to me.

Eddy lived with his mother, so he went straight home and asked if I could move in with them. I wanted to, but I had come to Belgium with a friend. Eddy thought it was Tanks, who I suppose he wouldn't have been happy with, but I told him it was Brian. The Planckaert's only had two bedrooms in their old house, so Eddy's sisters and husbands fixed up a room for us in an old cow shed.

Eddy's father had died when he was only six years old. He'd been in a car crash travelling home from a race that Willy had won. The family had struggled as their father had been hospitalised for a year before he died, and their mother was so badly injured that she could never work again.

Times were hard, but Willy turned professional and won the Green Jersey and two stages in the 1966 Tour de France. He rode every one of the post-Tour criteriums, and after them came home and put a suitcase full of money on the kitchen table. Their mother, Augusta, wept with pride for her son, and with pain because of the blows life had dealt them. Later, Willy contracted hepatitis, some say as a direct result of racing too much when he was young. He was never to reach the same racing level again, but the family had been saved.

4

The Planckaerts

Because I had won the Australian junior pursuit title before I set out for Belgium, I was selected for the World Junior Championships in Vienna. I told Eddy that I would come and live with them when I got back. The only problem was that I didn't have the money to get to Austria to compete. I was winning money, but once I'd paid for food, rent and to keep my bike in good working order, there was nothing left. Then one day a man called Scott Ramsey, who was to be the Australian team manager in Vienna called at the house in Ghent.

Scott's family had a private hospital in Queensland and they were all crazy about bike racing, but I told him I wouldn't be going to Vienna as I hadn't enough money. Next day he returned with an air ticket. Another Angel, exactly when I needed one?

I hadn't ridden the track for six months, and I certainly didn't have a track bike with me, but Tanks gave me the lend of his. I asked the Australian six-day star Danny Clarke, who lived in Ghent, if I could borrow of a pair of wheels, but he said he didn't have enough to lend me any. Of course he had enough, but Danny is known for being as tight as a fish's arse.

Once in Vienna I decided to focus on the road race first, then think about the track. Unfortunately there was a crash in the last kilometre of the road race, and I got caught up in it. I finished 20th and the Belgian Ronny Van Holen won, someone I beat normally every week.

There was an old school friend riding on the Australian team in Vienna, Tom Sawyer. He was the National Kilometre Champion, and after the Worlds he moved to Ghent to live at Rosa de Snerk's with 'Smelly' de Longville. Tom was in the same boat as me – no food and no money – but another rider on the team, Kenrick Tucker, the sprint champion, had an open cheque book from his home city, Rockhampton. Kenrick would go into a restaurant, eat one main course of Wiener Schnitzel, then order another and sneak it out to me and Tom.

The pursuit was my first track event, but qualifying was the day after the road race and I was still sore from my crash. It was also the first time I'd ridden a track bike in six months. I didn't even get a warm up. I was ninth in the qualifying time trial, one place outside qualifying for the quarter-finals.

Next was the points race. I won my heat, and in the final there were three of us on equal points at the bell for the last lap. It was a small, 250-metre track, very difficult to pass on when going flat out, so first at the bell would probably win maximum points one lap later. I was third at the bell, and third in the race, but I had a bronze medal at the Worlds!

Tom rode the kilometre, but hit every one of the sandbags they put on the inside of the track to make sure you ride the correct distance, on every one of the four laps that made up the 1,000 metres. I was watching in the stand, pissing myself laughing. I felt a bit guilty. But it was so funny: Tom was so nervous, too nervous to even hold his line.

Kenrick made the quarter-finals of the sprint, but his father would only let him ride an 86-inch gear when the Russian, Kopylev, was doing 10.8 seconds for the 200 metres in training, and quite necessarily using a big gear to do it.

Kenrick lost his quarter-final to Kopylev, who went on to become World Champion. Tom and I secretly changed Kenrick's gear up to 88 inches for the run-off for fifth, which he won. His father was furious.

After our efforts in Vienna, Scot Ramsey drove me back to Belgium and, with Brian, I moved into the Planckaert's. It was the start of my apprenticeship as a professional cyclist. The Planckaert boys were hard men, true Flandrians. Everything they did, everything they ate, was with the thought of being tougher and stronger. Strength was their family creed.

Brian lived with me, but he raced most days and had his own life with the amateurs. Every day when we weren't racing Eddy and I trained with Walter. We always used the same 100-kilometre undulating circuit, and never rode side by side, it was always doing turns, one kilometre on the front and swing off to let the next one set the pace. Racing with the juniors in Belgium the biggest gear you were allowed to use was 52 x 15. When we trained with Walter, we never changed out of that gear. Racing with the juniors was easy by comparison.

After training, Eddy and I washed in a bucket because there was no bathroom in his mother's house. Sometimes I was allowed to shower at Walter's. Eddy worked in the afternoons for a gardening firm, and he got me a job there as well. He taught me how to mow grass so that the lines were straight. Eddy didn't need to work, but did so because his brothers said it was good for him. It taught him the value of money and, I suppose, what other people had to do to earn it.

In the races we continued to clean up, always finishing Eddy first and me second. In my first year in Belgium I won one race, and was second 39 times. One time there was a special race where the organiser paid start money to the first ten finishers in the Belgian championships. Of course I had been ineligible for that payment, but Walter said he would give me the equivalent of $100 if I beat Eddy. Naturally he didn't tell Eddy.

At the start Eddy told me to attack, because the rest would watch him. Then he planned to jump across to me and we would be away. So once we got going I attacked and, just like he said they would, they watched him. I got a good lead, then looking behind me I saw Eddy attacking. There were some good riders in that race and it took him about four or five tries to get away.

At this point I had a lead of about 200 metres over Eddy, but $100 was a lot of money, so I really put the hammer down. Eddy got to about 50 metres behind me and began to yell out for me to wait, but I just kept going. Finally in one last, all-out effort Eddy caught me, and when he did he was furious.

I kept quiet and even attacked him on the last lap, but my saddle broke and Eddy won – again. When we got home all hell broke out. I didn't want to drop Walter in it because he had been good to me, so I made out that I didn't understand what Eddy was going on about. Years later that story still livens up the dinner table when we all get together.

Eddy's mother and his sisters looked after me like I was a fourth son. After all they had been through there was no place for sentimentality, but I had a warm safe home, although at times it was lonely. Brian was often away and my Flemish was minimal. The other English speakers at the house in Ghent had at least been someone for me to talk to, someone to share with. Eddy had his own life and would often be at his girlfriend's. I tried to live in my own world, but it was inevitable that the homesickness began to creep over me again.

Eventually, at the end of September, it was time to go home because the racing season was drawing to a close in Belgium. But I didn't really have a home. My father was in a clinic drying out for the fourth or fifth time. I got my bed back at Frank's place and started work on a building site to get the money to return to Europe the following year.

I visited my father in the clinic, and gave him a nice watch I had won in a race. I couldn't let go of the past, but I did feel for him; he was still my dad. He died in October 1995, alone in the apartment he lived in. His neighbours found his body after three days; all he was wearing was my watch.

My father

I went back to Belgium and to Eddy's alone in 1978. This time I was invited to live in the house with Eddy and his mother, sharing Eddy's bed. With the Planckaert's nothing is taboo, and Eddy had grown up sleeping with his brothers. I only had a sister and wasn't used to contact with males. Eddy would always end up with his arm or leg draped over me during the night. At first I didn't know how to react, but that was based on my own judgments of what was right; for Eddy it was the most normal thing in the world.

Eventually I lost my inhibitions and we had a lot of fun. We used to play this toughening-up game where we stripped off our clothes and flicked at each other with rolled up towels. For every ten hits on him I got 50 back. Our bodies would be covered with welts.

Eddy, being a year older that me, could now race with the amateurs, and he stopped working in the afternoon. Willy and Walter had conceded that, with the longer distances he was now racing, he needed more training and more rest. I carried on at the gardening and racing with the juniors, but I was older and wiser and won ten races, and finished second 25 times.

In the races I had fine-tuned a money-making scheme. Once a break formed, various riders would come up to me and ask if they could win, because they knew I was the strongest. They would promise me their prize money for this, and sometimes I said yes to two or three different riders. Then at the finish I would sprint anyway. If I won then great, but if I lost, one of those I'd made a deal with would win and I would still get the first-place cash. I made enough from racing and working to pay my board, keep my bike in working order, and still have some left over to make life relatively easy.

One rider I raced with a lot was Paul Haghedooren. Paul was a short, stocky, bespectacled rider who could race as hard as me, and he won a stage of the Kellog's Tour of Britain in 1987. We often took off at the start, and usually I had the upper hand at the finish. One race we rode in 1978 was the Junior Championship of Flanders. Greg Lemond was riding, and the world points race champion, Kenny De Martelaere, plus the Belgian champion. Paul and I got away not long after the start and lapped the field, on a four-kilometre circuit, with me winning. Paul never minded that, me winning.

A few years later as professionals in 1986, Paul and I got away together two laps from the end of a race in Zwevezele. I was with the Panasonic team, he was with Lotto and he was the Belgian Professional Champion by then. We rode like we did as juniors, neither holding back and with one lap to go we were holding the bunch of 200 riders at 100 metres. We made a deal that the winner would pay the other $500, so win or loose we would both make money. That way we both worked as hard as each other and managed to hold off the bunch, with me running out the winner.

Paul died from a heart attack during the winter of 1997, while playing football with some friends. There were a lot of people at his funeral, famous people from all walks of life and a lot of bike riders. I saw Paul's father from a distance in the church, our eyes met and for a moment there was a sparkle of recognition, him remembering me and his son as boys. Paul and I hardly ever had what I would call a conversation, such is the brotherhood of cycling.

Winning a Belgian Junior Race – 1978

Greg Lemond was in Belgium for a lot of the summer of 1978. I can remember seeing him get out of a car full of people at one race. I had ridden there in the rain and was angry that he could have it so easy.

A few weeks later I went to a race at Ostend on the Belgian coast with a new friend, Rudy Dhaenens, and his father. Rudy was a year younger than me, and held me in awe a bit. Lemond was there again and I got away with him, but he never passed me once during the race to do his share of work at the front.

In the last lap I said to Lemond that I would put him in the barriers if he tried to sprint. At 200 metres out he did try, but I moved across the road and didn't give him an inch of space. He was crying out that he'd fall, so I just allowed him breathing space as we rolled across the line with me winning and everybody in the crowd asking why we hadn't sprinted. Looking back, Greg was a good kid; it was me who was the pain in the arse.

The Junior World Championships that year were held in America, the track racing at Trexlertown and the road race in Washington. Unlike the previous year I had enough money to go, but had trouble getting selected, because I hadn't raced in the selection events. They were like that then, the Australian federation. But once again the Ramsey family came to the rescue. They threatened to pull the prizes they donated to the national championships, and not to manage the junior team, if I wasn't selected. Since they were funding their own trip to America, sanity prevailed and the federation relented. I was in.

I bought a cheap air ticket to New York from Icelandair, which meant I had to fly from Luxembourg, and the organizer of the championships, Jack Simes, agreed to meet me at JFK airport and drive me to Trexlertown. Unfortunately, I didn't realise that being 18 years old I needed a special visa to enter the US.

Eddy dropped me off at the train station in Ghent and off I went to Luxembourg. Then at check-in they said I couldn't travel, because I didn't have the special visa. Being Saturday the embassies were all closed and I had to get a hotel for two nights, which blew my budget.

Still, come Monday I got my visa and set off to America, with no money now, and no knowledge of the address where I was staying.

Of course Jack Simes thought I wasn't coming by then, so he wasn't there to meet me, but I did have his phone number. Because I had no money and no place to stay the US immigration wouldn't let me into the country. I tried ringing the number on reverse charges to get Jack to come over and sort everything out, but he wasn't in and his father, not recognising the number calling, wouldn't accept the charges. Stalemate. I was almost crying at my predicament.

Eventually an older woman (older! everyone looked older to me then) overheard what was going on and took pity on me, giving me a coin to make the call. That worked, and Jack eventually arrived to pick me up, although by that time I had missed the first round of the pursuit.

Next up was the points race. Two days travelling and on a borrowed bike, but I still won my heat. The other heat winner was Kenny De Martelaere, who lived near where I did in Belgium. Before the final we were warming up and I told Kenny that I had no money, even though I still had two weeks in the US to go before I could use my cheap ticket to get back to Belgium. Straightaway he offered to give me the cash but, too proud to take a gift, I said I'd help him in the final and he would pay me for that. In the end he was a class above us that night and won without any help, or the need to pay anyone. I ended up with second place, but still without enough money to last out my stay.

The Australian team took a bus to Washington. It was a one-way ride, so before the road race I was crying with fear about what was going to happen to me with ten days to go before I could fly back, and no way of getting to New York for the flight. It was time for another angel.

Luckily there was one in Washington, a guy called Mac who had raced in Belgium the year before. He arranged with his parents to take me back to his place in North Carolina. I didn't ride well in the race – my emotions were all over the place – but afterwards we drove back with Mac's mother, and Mac got me a job for a week sweeping the floors in the factory where he worked. It ended up being the most fun week I'd ever had. I made some money, and we even rode a race at the weekend where Mac arranged for someone who was going back to New York to drop me at JFK.

How is it, though, that things fit together sometimes so perfectly just when they need to? I have a feeling it happens when you let it, or when you just surrender to the situation, maybe even when you just give up trying to make things happen. You have probably had the experience where the phone rings and somebody comes to mind; you pick up the phone and it's them. Or you have a chance meeting with somebody you know 10,000 kilometres from home, or a guardian angel arrives in your life at exactly the time you need them to.

It's called 'synchronicity', and usually in our busy lives we are oblivious to it, because we try to make our lives happen rather than letting them unfold. Our heads are always busy with 'stuff'. It is that 'stuff' which obscures the signals of synchronicity we receive. I don't know how it works, I only know that it is there, like the phone call. We think, 'Wow!' when that happens, but synchronicity is there all the time; we are just not aware of it. It's like a signpost with a message or a direction, or it comes as a gut feeling. James Redfield in his book, *The Secret of Shambala*, said that we need not just to be aware of synchronicity, but look for it, be ready for it, expect it and prepare for it.

It was a long trip back to Europe, with a lot to keep me thinking. Eventually I arrived back in Ghent, where I put my medal around my neck, hung my bag on the handlebars of my bike and rode the 20 kilometres from St Peter's station back to the Planckaert's in Nevele.

When I walked into the kitchen, Eddy and his mother were talking and Walter was reading the newspaper. They looked up, asked me how I'd done. 'Second,' I said, showing them the medal, and they went right back to what they were doing. No questions about my trip, nothing about my experiences. They weren't uninterested because I'd 'only' come second, but because it had nothing to do with Flemish cycling. That was the Plankaerts' world – it revolved around the Tour of Flanders and Paris–Roubaix; the Tour de France hardly existed, never mind junior track racing in America. I felt a little sad but, looking back, they could have had no conception of the experiences I'd just been through.

5

Alaric Gayfer

I've already told you about how hard Eddy Planckaert and I trained. We lived like professionals, even though we were still juniors. We trained every day, no matter what the weather was like. After each session we would wash, have a meal, then get in a short sleep before we went to work. Every night we were in bed by nine o'clock. We were totally committed, totally dedicated, and that commitment and dedication brought us results.

Unfortunately though, in cycling, good results can be put down to another reason – drugs. Where we worked at the gardening, our success sometimes brought taunts from the older men, and even more so if we didn't win. They would say, 'What happened, did you run out of tablets?'

'Good vitamins' is what they called drugs in Belgium. I'd heard the term a lot the previous year. Brian and his mates were always talking about 'good vitamins'. In Australia I had never even heard of drugs in cycling, but they were part of the scene in Belgium. So much so that some people were convinced that Eddy and I were on them. It was the only way they could explain how good we were. But they didn't see how much work we did.

One weekend, when racing with the juniors, I won a race in Ronse by five minutes on the Saturday, then lapped the field to win again in Nevele on the Sunday. After each race they had a doping control and I was tested. Someone was convinced that I was doped and they were out to get me, but I passed both tests.

I could have got hold of drugs if I'd wanted to. I wasn't naïve. I remember having 'Decca Durabolin', an anabolic steroid, suggested to me before I went to the World Championships in America. The person who suggested it to me was older than me, but almost as soon as he'd said it he said, 'No, you don't need that'. I still wonder if he had my health in mind, or if he was worried that *he* might get caught.

The rumours though were constant. Not only about me but about other riders I rode with. If someone was going well, they were taking drugs. If they went badly, it was too much or too little drugs. Decca Durabolin, which everybody just called 'Decca', had the side effect of making your face look fat. So everyone with a fat face was automatically on 'Decca'.

Still, I was oblivious to the whole scene. It was like being aware of music in the background but not listening to it. I was the same when I turned pro: it was all around me, but not only did I not get deeply involved in it, most of the time I didn't even see it.

Even late on in my career I wasn't always aware of what was going on. I can remember the first of the after-Tour criteriums in 1992, held in Aalst in Belgium. After getting changed and leaving the changing rooms, one of my Tulip Computers team-mates asked me, 'Did you see all the guys charging up in there?' I looked at him, dumbfounded, and said, 'No, where?' Then he told me how guys were slipping a hypodermic under the skin at the top of their thighs as they adjusted their shorts, or doing it in the upper arm as they pretended to rub on Eau de Cologne with a face cloth.

The apparently stupid part of that scene in Aalst was that it was a 100-kilometre criterium But you have to understand that this mentality had been with cycling almost from the start. Guys were using stuff like strychnine and cocaine in the earliest races. Then after the Second World War amphetamines became the drug of choice. It meant that the whole scene was riddled, but no-one's contract depended on the race in Aalst.

At best, taking drugs in those races was a way of easing the mental pressure of racing three weeks in the Tour de France and following that with 30 criteriums. Or it was a joke, it was fun, a buzz, no different from a beer or a coffee. That was the attitude; it was as commonplace as that, just like naughty kids experimenting with beer or cigarettes in the park, and regarded as nothing more serious or shameful than that. I certainly didn't give it much thought.

Maybe a lot of what was going on went over my head because of the attitude I'd had since I started racing. I was only interested in what I was doing at the time. For example, when I was living at Eddy's house, Willy and Walter Planckaert often asked me to go with them to races in France, but it didn't interest me. I didn't want to watch pros racing, or anybody else for that matter, I just wanted to race myself. I did once go to a track meeting in France with the Planckaerts. I had to, they'd asked so many times that another refusal would have offended them.

With Eddy now racing with the amateurs, I teamed up with Rudy Dhaenens during 1978. He was a really nice guy, and at the end of the season I helped him win the race his supporters' club put on. I didn't charge him any money for it either, which shows the regard I had for Rudy.

But friendships apart, I was really looking forward to going back to Australia. To get there I had to take the boat to England, where I stayed overnight with the family of an English friend I'd met while he was racing in Belgium during the summer, Alaric Gayfer.

Alaric's father was the editor of *Cycling Weekly* magazine, and the family lived in Hackney. I stayed with them for one night and next morning Alaric's mother said she would give me a lift to the underground station, so I could get the train for the airport. But when we got to the station I told her I had no money for the fare. She was very good about it and let me have five pounds, but said it was a loan. I can't remember now if I ever paid her back, but I really appreciated her kindness and her treating me like an adult, saying it was a loan.

I don't know why I'd waited until the last minute before telling her I had no money. I was too proud to say until I was desperate, I suppose. It was typical of me in those days, though. I lived by the seat of my pants. It's funny, but as you get older that attitude disappears. You account for every possibility and plan accordingly, but at the same time you lose some of the spontaneity from your life.

Back in Australia my mother had separated from my father. She had rented a house with her sister, so I moved in with them. It was wonderful to be together again in something like a family but, after years of trauma with my father, my mother was really an emotional mess. On top of that, she still had to provide for herself and my sister so she was back doing double shifts at the hospital. That situation didn't help her condition.

That Aussie summer I worked for a builder, who was also a bike rider, Hilton Clarke, or 'The Monster' as we all used to call him. I rode my bike, sometimes 50 kilometres, to work, worked the whole day on the site, digging and lifting. Then I would ride home again. After a hard season in Europe, it was too much.

Added to that, I raced on the track and won four Gold Medals in the Oceania Games, which were held in Australia that year. They weren't hard medals to win, but on top of the work I was doing and the tiredness I'd brought back with me from Belgium, I was just pushing myself into a downward spiral of over-training.

By the time I took the 'plane back to Belgium I was tired, and I knew it. I was now 19 and could race with the amateurs. They rode longer races, requiring more effort and even more dedication in training, and certainly more rest. I had some good results, like fourth in a major sage-race in Luxembourg, but I couldn't win. I didn't have that extra edge. It really upset Eddy Planckaert. He was turning pro later on in the year, and wanted me to go with him, but I just didn't have the results.

I had ridden in Luxembourg with a mixed team of English-speaking riders, and four of us left after the race to go and ride the Tour of the Loire Valley. One of the riders was Alaric Gayfer, who had an old Peugeot car, so we loaded our bikes onto the roof and off we went; me, Alaric, Tom Sawyer and Dave Brotherton. The latter two Aussies like me.

I finished the race in second place overall and we thought we would get our money at the end, like you do in Belgium. But no, the organisers said that they would pay our prizes to our cycling federations and we had to claim the money back from them. We didn't even get anything to eat at the after-race presentation.

Now we had a problem: we either had enough money to eat, or enough to get back to Belgium. We couldn't afford both. Then on the motorway towards Paris the car broke down at a service station. It was past midnight but the mechanic at the service station tried to help us get the thing going, only it wouldn't. Eventually it became obvious that the costs of repair would exceed the value of the car, so Alaric took off the number plates, got our bikes down off the roof and we set off riding to the railway station, leaving his old Peugeot behind.

Eventually we arrived in Paris, having been thrown off two trains for not having a ticket. There we pooled our remaining money and had enough to buy a long loaf and a bottle of Coke. We split the loaf and ate our first food since before the race the previous day. They wouldn't let us on the train for Belgium, but negotiating and pleading eventually got them to agree to bill us in Belgium and they let us on board. We spent the rest of the journey hallucinating about trips to McDonalds and what we would eat there.

Back in Belgium Alaric, Dave and Tom helped me get my one and only race victory that year, in a criterium in Deinze. Alaric died towards the end of 2004, just before I started writing this book, after a long battle with a brain tumour. He lived in America by then, where he was a well respected cycling coach. He wasn't a really great bike rider, although he was good, and especially so when he was younger, I understand. But, like his father, he loved cycling and he loved cyclists. He found his true métier in being a coach, and it was Alaric who trained the USA's 2000 Olympic Sprint Champion, Marty Nothstein.

The Planckaerts loved Alaric for his dry sense of humour, and they gave him an old BMW that had belonged to Eddy's brother-in-law. Alaric put another 100,000 kilometres on its clock before he had to leave it somewhere in Germany.

It's not only the champions that make cycling such a great sport. Often it's the people like Alaric, who hold cycling in their hearts and help others aspire to greatness. We lost Rudy Dhaenens a few years ago, too. He was killed in a car crash. No wonder I am so aware of my own mortality with my friends disappearing like they have.

Shortly after my win in Deinze I got sick. I had been pushing myself too hard for too long and I went down with an infection. At the Planckaert's house we used to drink water from a hand-drawn well. There was a pig farm opposite their house and effluent must have seeped into the water table. Apparently the Planckaerts were immune to the bacteria but, with my lowered resistance, I wasn't. What did worry them, though, was if Eddy should catch something from me. Willy had hepatitis when he was young and it had ruined his career, so they made me up a bed in the front room and moved me out from being with Eddy.

After taking some antibiotics I felt better, but racing was a different proposition. I went with Eddy to my first race since I'd been ill and was dropped on the second lap. People who knew me, and knew how good I'd been, were laughing at me. There were plenty of jokes about drugs, and how I was finished. Even in the changing rooms some of the other riders were making insinuations. I remember Eddy coming in there after the race, and me just breaking down in tears. He said things would get better but, in truth, that phase of my life when winning was easy had gone. I was never the same bike rider again.

I couldn't race any more at that time. To keep me from being on my own too much Eddy's sister, Anita, and her husband, Carlos, took me out to places, but eventually I decided that it was no good. I had to go home and I wouldn't be coming back. It was over.

Eddy took me to the airport, dropping me off at the entrance to the terminal. Things had changed between us and he was cold, although I know now that he was only trying to protect his heart. The following year he got married to his long-time girlfriend, Christa, and he wrote to me, asking me to come back for the wedding. I told him that I couldn't as I had no money because my mother was sick and couldn't work regularly. Eddy sent me two boxes of new cycling kit, so that I could sell them and raise some extra cash, but I had more pressing matters. I needed that cash to keep everything together and pay some bills.

Back in Australia I moved in with my mother and sister again. My health was still terrible so I visited the doctor, who put me in the infectious diseases hospital for two weeks, where they did all sorts of tests. But, in the end, all they did was fill me up with antibiotics – about six months supply.

I went back to work for another builder friend, John Simpson. My first job was to dig out a room beneath a house that had been built on stilts on a hillside. To make matters worse, I had to shift out everything I had dug with a wheelbarrow. Every time I came out into the light, pushing that wheelbarrow, I could see in the distance the shape of the Dandenong Mountains, my favourite place to train. It was 1980, Olympic year, and I should have been there with the Australian team, but all I could do was turn around with my wheelbarrow and descend back into the dark. My heart ached to be a bike rider with every shovel full of dirt I put into that barrow. Sometimes it still aches to be a bike rider, even today.

After my career I took a spiritual path, trying to discover who I really was, and I found that the only thing that I wouldn't be prepared to give up in my life was my bike. When I thought about life without it I got scared. I found out that cycling was who I am. My bike had been my companion since I was ten years old. I cherished it and looked after it with my heart, and in return it didn't let me down. That I guess is the attachment, why cycling has been my life. It still is, even in the years since my retirement I still go riding when it is minus five degrees Celsius.

In the years since I stopped racing many people have made derogatory remarks about me because I still enjoyed riding my bike. Some former riders thought I was crazy to still be riding. I have even wondered if they are right, and questioned why I did it. But then I read in Lance Armstrong's book where he described riding three times up the Hautacam mountain climb in the rain and cold just so that he could commit every metre of it to memory. If he could do that, was I crazy to still love my bike and love riding it?

Taking all the antibiotics I took played havoc with my intestinal tract, and my physical condition became so low I was scared I would end up with cancer. I tried to train, but if I rode to work I didn't have enough energy to dig. In desperation I entered a race, but it was no good – I was dropped at the halfway point.

Then one night I was visiting Frank Cunningham at his house, when Peter Brotherton called in. Peter was a frame builder, who had been an Olympic rider with the British team at Melbourne in 1956, and had also won two silver medals in the pursuit at the World Championships. He had been offered a place on the lucrative European Six-Day track racing circuit, but a bad knee injury meant that he had to refuse it.

He was in Australia when this happened, and his wife was back in London. So he wrote her a letter telling her that she could either take the boat now to meet him, or wait until spring when he would come back for her, but they were emigrating to Australia.

Peter's knee injury set off his search to understand how the body worked, how it healed itself and regenerated. His nickname in

Australia was 'the Professor', so learned and respected had he become. He'd helped a lot of people and, when we discussed my problems that night at Frank's, he invited me to go and stay with him for a week, and he would show me how to get myself well again.

At first, I didn't take him up on his offer, but a few weeks later I went to see him about a new bike frame and we got talking again about my health. Eventually he persuaded me, and I told him that I would be down the following week.

First, though, I had to sort out my mother. She had come out of hospital from yet another operation and the bills were piling up because she couldn't work. I used the money I was saving up for a car, and sold the clothes Eddy had sent me, to sort out the bills. I stayed with her for two weeks until she got mobile, then told her I was going to Peter's. She didn't want me to go and I felt responsible for her, but my bike was my life and Peter had given me the hope of a way back. I was torn between a rock and a hard place and, after a heated argument with my mother, I left for a one-week stay at Peter's which turned into nearly two years.

I felt guilty about leaving my mother. I tried to care for her, did things for her, cleaning and cooking, trying to make her life easier. I have done the same with a lot of other people, including my wife. I think it's because deep down I felt rejected by my mother when she chose my father over me before I went to Belgium. That hurt, and I have never wanted anybody to hurt me in the same way again, so I've tried hard to please. Not always with success.

Peter Brotherton was my life's guardian angel. I never would have got back to racing if it hadn't been for him. As soon as I arrived at his house he put me on a regime of riding, working and only eating what he prescribed.

Every day he made me ride to work, even if it was a round trip of 100 kilometres. He and his wife, Pam, would get me up at 5.30 am; she would make my packed lunch of mint tea and alfalfa sandwiches, while Peter made me a breakfast of freshly ground seeds with yoghurt and honey, all washed down with grapefruit juice.

I was still working on the building sites, and did I get my leg pulled by the bricklayers? Alfalfa sandwiches and mint tea in the homophobic Australia of the early 80s, I ask you? But I stuck to it. Peter introduced me to the pioneers of the health food movement through the books he had. Men like Paul Bragg, John Kellogg, Norman Walker and Paavo Airola.

One book I read was by Ann Wigmore, who extolled the virtues of wheat grass juice. Every night when I walked into Peter's house my stomach would do back-flips at the smell of wheat grass juice, and it was all I could do to hold the stuff down, but I believed totally in what Peter was doing.

Paul Bragg made the biggest impression on me, with his fasting. Four times a year he fasted on water for a week to ten days, and once a week he did without food for 24 to 36 hours; and he was a rock of a man. So I decided I should have a go at fasting. At first it was torture: the first fast I did was for 36 hours, and all I could think about was McDonalds. Then, over the following weeks, I got more confidence and found ways of keeping my mind occupied, and off thoughts of food. I did a two-day, then a three-day fast. My energy rose and I was bursting with new life.

At first Peter wouldn't let me race, because he said I wasn't strong enough. But after only four months of fasting and eating well I was ready. I started on the track and won a silver medal in the National Pursuit Championships behind former World Points Race Champion, Gary Sutton. It was a very close race and we were level at the bell, but Gary produced a blistering last lap to just beat me. After that I was straight into the Australian road season and won just about everything there was to win, apart from the National Title.

But that was because I wasn't selected for the state team and didn't even go to the race. The selectors said they wouldn't pick me as they knew I was going back to Europe! Half the riders picked for the team wouldn't race because the selectors wanted them to pay half the price of their air ticket, so they didn't even have a full team. Yet they still didn't pick me.

I had a lot of trouble like that, back in those days. The following year was the Commonwealth Games, and even though I was getting top results in France, I didn't get selected. In fact, I heard a rumour that after I had won the amateur Grand Prix des Nations time trial in France by five minutes, the Commonwealth committee in Australia contacted the Cycling Federation and told them that they would pay for my ticket back to Australia for the Games in Brisbane. Yet they still wouldn't pick me, saying that I hadn't ridden the selection race, the National Championships, the previous year.

Towards the end of 1981 I started to back off a bit in my training. I had learned the hard way that rest was very important and wanted to be ready for my next adventure. The president of the club I was riding for in Australia was a Frenchman called Gerald George. He had a lot of contacts and had got me a place in the famous ACBB amateur team, which is based in Paris.

Many great riders had passed through their ranks on their way to becoming top professionals including, in the years just before I went, a lot of English-speakers. But even more than that, ACBB was the amateur squad for the legendary Peugeot professional team, which had been home to some of the sport's greats, like Eddy Merckx, Tom Simpson and Bernard Thévenet. ACBB had also produced Paul Sherwen, Graham Jones, Stephen Roche, Robert Millar, Sean Yates and the man whose footsteps I was following in – the greatest of all Australian riders – Phil Anderson.

Australia has produced some amazing riders, both on the road and on the track. World and Olympic Champions many of them. The country is still doing it today with Robbie McEwen, Stuart O'Grady and Michael Rodgers, to name but three. Quite understandably, there is a lot of debate about which one of all the great riders in Australian cycling history is the best, but because I regard European professional cycling as the top of the sport, the best for me by far is Phil. I raced with him for ten years as a pro, twice in the same team with Peugeot and Panasonic. If I looked up to anybody during those years it was to Phil.

6

Phil Anderson

I first met Phil Anderson while racing with the Hawthorn club in Melbourne, when I was 15 years old. The president of that club was a man called Ted Sanders, and he and his wife, Joan, were terrific bike fans. Nothing was too much for them to do for a cyclist, and there was always some rider from a different part of the country staying at their house. On top of that, their sons, David and John, were good riders, who both raced in Europe.

Ted and Joan took me and my mate, Tom Sawyer, to races all over the place. The other two in that car were Phil Anderson and his mate, Peter Darbyshire. Phil and Peter were two years older than me and went to a private school, whereas Tom and I went to the roughest technical school, and I'll never forget the games of 'I-spy' we played in the car with those two brainy kids. One time Peter came out with the word 'facetious'. I had never even heard of it, never mind knowing what it meant.

One trip we all went on was to ride a series of track carnivals in South Australia. From Melbourne the whole trip must have taken in about 2,000 kilometres. Phil had by this time been dubbed 'Phil the Dill' by me and Tom, although we were wise enough not to call him that to his face. Not because we didn't want to hurt his feelings, but because Phil was also in the wrestling team.

He was a real hard case. During the trip Phil must have touched down (crashed) at least four times, and he had skin off everywhere. In the back of the car I took great delight every time we went round a corner in leaning on 'Darbs' who in turn had to lean on Phil, making him cry out in pain. It didn't even matter which side he sat on, because he was raw on both sides from crashes.

The racing was so funny, watching Phil, this 'goose' kid, riding the D grade senior events and touching down again and again. He crashed in almost every race he rode, or it seemed like it at the time.

Tom and I loved that. It wasn't callous; it was just us getting the evener on these posh kids.

Looking back, those trips were a good part of my youth. I felt safe and loved with Ted and Joan. Ted had been a minister in the church and both of them were people of compassion. Joan would either make us all sandwiches for the ride or, if we stopped for a meal, Ted would pay. Ted always paid – for everything. It was like we were his kids, and for me it felt good.

One Saturday night there had been a fight at home, and my father had come into my room and hit me over the head with a bedside lamp. The impact caused a cut above my eye. Next day we had a track meeting, and the effort of racing and pressure from my crash-hat opened the wound up again, making if bleed profusely and forcing me to abandon the race. Ted and Joan were there to tend the wound and patch me up, but they never asked about its origin, although they knew. That was what they were like: they didn't want to embarrass me.

But getting back to Phil, even though we took the Micky out of him and he was ungainly on his bike, there was something about him that had already caught my eye. Even as a kid, he had a depth you couldn't fathom. He had the will to carry on, no matter what happened. He would crash, get up and do it again, without even a whimper. Even with me taunting him in the back of the car, he always took it with good humour.

Phil had grown up with a single mother, who had come to Australia shortly after he was born. When I first knew him he was having trouble with his step-father, not that he ever talked about it. There was a deep-seated determination within Phil, something motivated him really deep down. You couldn't see it, but you could feel it. It was what gave Phil a brute animal quality. Women even called him 'Phil the Thrill'.

Shortly after our road trip around South Australia, I left for Europe and Phil went on to win the 1978 Commonwealth Games Road Title. Then, with the help of Gerald George, he left for France, and one year later turned professional for Peugeot.

I remember sitting at the back of Peter Brotherton's house a couple of years later, trying to recover my health, and hearing that

47

Phil was in the Yellow Jersey, leading the Tour de France. I thought about us in the back of Ted and Joan's car and wanted to speed up time so I could catch him up. I had just won the Dulux Tour in New Zealand, only the second Australian ever to win it. Phil was the other.

Later, we raced together for a year with Peugeot and two years with Panasonic. We trained together and I watched and learned from the master. He had a big influence on me by the way he did things. He was so professional and so motivated. Even Peter Post, in later years, said that Anderson was the most professional rider he'd ever met.

He always ate good food, always looked after himself. I went to a criterium with him once, soon after I turned pro and he had a compressor that worked off the car battery in his boot to pump up his bike tyres. He would also travel to every criterium with two sets of wheels – one with tyres for the dry, and one with tyres for the wet.

I would have given my career to Phil, but like so many champions he was totally focused on himself. Anyway, Phil could do it without my help. There aren't many team leaders who need a helper by their side and value them for years. Domestiques, as the riders who help the stars are known, are a disposable asset.

To explain the relationship I'll tell you about some of the races we rode. I didn't come up to Phil's ankles as a rider, but it never stopped me trying to beat him if I could. One time I did beat him was in the prologue time trial of the Dauphiné Libéré. Phil was not happy, but next day it was my turn to be not happy as all the headlines said was that Phil had been beaten into second place; they didn't say who had beaten him.

Then in the 1987 Milan–San Remo I really learned the difference between what was expected of a leader and of a domestique, and it was Phil who taught me. I had been away in a very long break and attacked on the last climb but one, the Cipressa. Eric Maechler from Switzerland came with me and we stayed away until the Poggio, the last climb.

Halfway up the Poggio there is a straight bit where you can look down and see three or four sections of the switchback climb below you. Maechler looked down and saw Phil, my team-mate at Panasonic, attacking off the front of the group that was immediately behind us. In response, Maechler, who had been riding in 53x16, changed down on to the 15 sprocket (after 295 kilometres of riding!) and blew me off his wheel. The group caught me but not Maechler, who won with my team leader, the Belgian Eric Vanderaerden in second place, and I got the blame for him losing.

I have never spoken to Phil about what happened on that climb. I've never told anyone, in fact. I just let it ride. In 1991 we were in the Kellogg's Tour of Britain and ten of us, including Phil, got away on the first stage. I attacked at the one-kilometre banner and got a gap, but at a roundabout, with 300 metres to go, the lead car went left and I followed, only seeing at the last minute that the race direction sign pointed right. I slammed on my brakes, losing all my speed, and the first to pass me was Phil. I pushed on to his wheel and as I did so I knew exactly what I would do. With 200 metres left Phil kicked up the speed and I let him go, because I knew that the others would now have to come round me to chase Phil. The gap became five seconds by the finish line, a lead which Phil defended for five days to win the race.

Afterwards I heard that it was Phil who had chased me down after my attack with one kilometre to go. And I had given him the gap that allowed him to win the stage and the race. That is the difference between a champion and the rest. Champions have to win, no matter what it costs.

I have tremendous admiration for Phil Anderson as a cyclist. I saw him win races. I saw him decimate a field of the world's best riders. I saw him train. Tom Sawyer and I even named a hill after Phil here in Belgium. Before the Worlds in 1988 he did intervals up that hill, 17 times and it's a five minute climb. It will always be 'Phil's Hill'; he christened it with his sweat.

I am off for a run now with my mate, by coincidence another Phil. We are going to do 20 kilometres and do some sprints and a couple of block sessions. It'll be hard work, but I know the other Phil is back in Oz doing the same crazy shit as me, so it's OK.

7

Pete Longbottom

It was the eve of my return to Europe, and I was standing in the old house, a place Peter Brotherton owned next to his own. My dog Boofy, a black Labrador/Pointer cross, came and sat next to me, so I knelt down and put my arms around him.

I had found Boofy in a lost-dogs home; he was just six weeks old when I got him and he could fit into my slipper. Now he was as tall as my hip, had a shiny jet-black coat and there wasn't an ounce of fat on him. I ran him five kilometres a day, fed him on kangaroo meat and bean sprouts, and every night he slept on my bedroom floor with a blanket over him. Boofy knew what was happening, and as the tears rolled down my face I was sure that his heart was breaking, too. My cases were packed, standing ready; he could see them and he knew.

I thought we were alone, but then I heard a voice. 'You don't have to go, you know. You don't have to go for me.' It was Peter, and what he was trying to say was that I only had to leave if I really wanted to. Peter had wanted to become a professional – it was his dream – but his injured knee had stopped him. He needed me to know that I didn't have to go to live his dream for him. I had to do it for myself.

And right there in that room, on that night, in my head I probably didn't want to leave and go to Europe. But then I thought how bad, how lost I had felt when I was forced to abandon cycling and come home. I knew deep down in my heart that I had to go and race. It was where I was being guided. Racing was the breath of my life; it made my soul sing and my spirit soar. The pull TO GO was bigger than me, bigger than reason even.

When I arrived in Brussels I was welcomed like a long-lost son by Eddy Planckaert's sister, Anita, and her husband, Carlos. I had arranged to spend two weeks with them in Belgium during January, before going on to Paris and joining my new team, ACBB. It was great to see everyone again. Eddy was a pro by then and had already won a stage in the Tour de France. I borrowed a bike and trained with his team, and I made quite an impression on their manager by riding on the front of the group with an Englishman, Steve Jones. Eddy was very proud of me, boasting about my prowess as a cyclist. He had more confidence in me than I had in myself at that moment. It was also great to be back in Flanders. The rain, the cold, all the mud and shit on the roads, the smell of sweat, the swish of tyres and the sound of shifting gears, the smells of the fields and animals all spoke to me of security. It was a place where I knew I was safe, where there were people who cared about me.

Yet, looking back now, even in Belgium I never felt really settled. The funny thing was that when I was in Australia I missed Belgium, and when I was in Belgium I missed Australia. My mother said that I would always be torn between two countries, and she was right.

Unfortunately, I wasn't with Eddy and his family for long. Soon the day came to take the train to Paris, and I felt the same sense of loss that I'd felt a hundred times before, and would feel many more times in the future, as I travelled the world to different bike races.

It has been a strange life, I've always had something compelling me to move on, to experience things, while at the same time I haven't wanted to leave behind the things I was familiar with. Sometimes, it felt like I was being torn in two, but then one day it all came out.

After I finished my cycling career, I went on a trip to India. I arrived in Delhi and was staying the night in a monastery there, while waiting for a train north into the foothills of the Himalayas. I was there trying to explore my spirituality, at least that is what I'd told myself I was doing. In truth, I didn't really know why I'd gone. But, looking back, I realise it was the same guiding force, a bigger force than my own free will, that compelled me to do so many things in my life that had sent me to India.

I'd only been there a couple of hours when a feeling of utter loneliness came over me. I just couldn't face being on my own and away from the people I loved anymore, and I began to panic. I took my pack and got a rickshaw back to the airport. I thought that maybe

I could get on the same flight and go back home, but it was full, so I had to return to the monastery.

I have never felt such despair before. It was like all the loneliness of my life was coursing through my body, and I was racked with grief at my lost childhood, my parent's bitter relationship and the utter despair of never having known what it felt like to be really safe. I fell to my knees by the side of my bed and cried for hours, until the sheets were soaking wet. I prayed; I begged for the pain and the load of this loneliness to be taken from me. I wasn't conscious of what I was doing; it was just total desperation.

By the time I regained some kind of control over myself I had missed my train north, so I collapsed into that wet bed and fell fast asleep. I awoke a few hours later in the middle of the night, and immediately I felt it. Something had changed. Incredibly, I felt lighter. It was gone, the burden had been lifted. Those desperate moments in India were the culmination of my life experiences, and they had got me. I had tried, unconsciously, to race out the pain, to suffer it out so I couldn't feel the underlying hurt any more. But after I stopped racing there was no avenue for me; I couldn't avoid it by adding pain anymore, artificial pain, and the whole scary monster of my life, the monster I'd repressed for years, had got me.

* * * * *

Arriving in Paris back in 1982 was another lonely and scary moment. I managed to get to the building where the club was based, but it was all in darkness and there was no one there to meet me. So I sat in the doorway, cold and hungry, wondering why I had left Belgium to come here.

Eventually the concierge arrived and let me into the building, directing me to a small room where there was a bed. I asked him in English where I could get some food, but I didn't understand a word he said in reply. I felt really stupid, I had French lessons at school for two years, but I lived in a town of about 1000 people, just a few kilometres from Melbourne, and I couldn't see the point of learning French. Now I was paying for my laziness.

In Paris I was playing out a scenario that would be repeated over and over again throughout my life. I would be excited to leave for the next race, and the trip would go well. But once alone in my room, the same feeling would come over me. The same feeling as I felt that night in Paris, loneliness and wanting to be back with the people I loved.

When I was a pro and travelling to races, my wife used to make me sandwiches for the trip, even though there would be a meal on the plane, and within the team all our needs were catered for. But I never threw those sandwiches away; they represented my wife's love and care, and sometimes I ate them two days later when I was alone in my hotel room. It wasn't about the sandwiches; it was about the love I'd left behind.

Once as a child, when my mother was away working in the city, I had my tenth birthday and my father bought me some really beautiful leather football boots. Then a parcel arrived from my mother. I opened it and she'd bought me some plastic boots. My heart yearned for her, the love she'd put into buying and sending those boots. At school the kids laughed at me for wearing the plastic boots, but they were from her, from the heart, just like my wife's sandwiches.

All the foreigners who went through ACBB lived together in one apartment in Paris. There were four of us when I went: me, two Englishmen – Alan Gornall and Pete Longbottom – and an American, Karl Maxon. Pete had been there the year before, so he knew the ropes and arrived first so he could get the room with the double bed. Alan and I shared a smaller room, and Karl got the sofa bed in the living room.

Being obsessive about cleaning, I soon got the place organised. Well, actually, Alan and I used to do it all: he would do the kitchen and bathroom, while I did the floors and the beds. We were like minded, Alan and I. He was recovering from a broken leg and had a lot of pain, but he was very good at supporting me in races. If anything, Alan was more house-proud and domesticated than me, and we all called him 'mummy' because he could cook a great fruit pie.

Everyone had their own ways. Pete was a nice guy, but he used to hide his food under his bed. He was paranoid that somebody would eat it. Every morning he would go out and buy a long French loaf, which he would warm in the oven and eat with butter and jam and a cup of tea while reading *L'Équipe*, the French sports newspaper. I don't even know if he could read French, but he looked the part anyway.

Pete was also crazy about the Milk Race; he was always going on about it. It was, 'In the Milk Race this' and 'In the Milk Race that'. He loved it. He loved the hotels, the crowds. He even used to go on about the food the organisers handed up in Britain – mint cake, and some other cake he only got on the Milk Race.

He and I were often in the winning break together that year, but no matter what the team director told him to do, Pete would never attack, and he couldn't sprint. If there were four of us in a break Pete would finish fourth. He had a nose for reading a race and being in the right moves, and I think he would have made a great domestique in a pro team, but you need to win races as an amateur to become any kind of pro. Pete was killed in 1998, hit by a car while riding home from work in York through a dark English winter evening.

The club was a really professional set-up. I hadn't ever experienced anything like it at that stage of my career. As soon as we'd sorted ourselves out in the apartment, we all got our new bikes and clothing, and set off for a training camp in the South of France.

I won a race down there at Les Issambres, which was where the big boss of ACBB, Monsieur Wiegand, lived. So I'd scored some good points with him. Along with two other riders, he invited me to stay at his house. It was a privilege, but it also served to drive a wedge between me and the French guys in the club.

From the time we arrived you could feel the tension with the French riders. Every year only one or two riders from the club turned professional, and in the previous four years Paul Sherwen, Graham Jones, Phil Anderson, Stephen Roche, Sean Yates and John Herety had all passed their test and gone on to race with the big boys. The French didn't like that, they thought we were taking their places, but they could have remedied it by getting better results.

ACBB rode the biggest amateur races in France – we did all the classics and lots of stage races. But, I had the reputations of all those English-speakers who had gone before me to live up to. Stephen

Roche was the benchmark – he won 21 races in his year with the club. Phil Anderson was next with 17.

I tried to do what I could to follow them. In Paris–Roubaix for amateurs I finished fourth. There were two riders away, and I had them in sight until some level crossing barriers came down and stopped me. While I was waiting a group caught me and one of them outsprinted me for third. Eventually, though, the winner was disqualified for doping.

Walter Planckaert, who was by then a directeur sportif with the Splendor pro team, was at the finish in Roubaix, and he offered me a pro contract. It was a good deal – $2,000 US per month and an apartment rent-free. I was over the moon, but I told Walter I would call him back. I wanted to talk to Peter Brotherton in Australia first, but when I did Peter wasn't happy. He said it was too early to turn pro and advised me to go with my original plan, which was do a full year with ACBB and try to get a two-year contract with the Peugeot pro team. I pleaded with him, because I really wanted to ride for Walter, but Pete was right: I wasn't strong enough to be a pro yet, and needed a year of riding amateur stage races every other week to get that strength.

Life in Paris was hard though, and I think that was one of the reasons why I wanted to accept Walter's offer. I met nobody, and made no friends outside my cycling world. Parisians live at such speed, and everywhere you go people are in a hurry. In the supermarkets, post offices or on the trains, it's just push and shove and never a hello. It wasn't quite so bad for the English riders: they were close enough to home for the occasional trip back. My only treat was a weekly visit to the cinema and a piece (a piece!) of pizza on the way home.

But somehow I got by. I liked the guys I was sharing with, it was only Karl Maxon who didn't really fit in. He had a different way of thinking. For example, at one race he abandoned and rode 100 kilometres back to Paris without telling anyone what he was doing.

Of course, I didn't help the situation. I used to wind Karl up. I was like that in those days. One day we were all in the kitchen making dinner and Paul Sherwen, who was a pro with La Redoute by then and in Paris to prepare for the Bordeaux–Paris race, was staying with us. Paul was in the bathroom, and Karl had been getting on my nerves all day, but now I was provoking him. Things escalated and Karl, who was at the sink, suddenly turned and threw a six inch knife at me, just as Paul was entering the room. I dodged it, but it nearly hit Paul. After that Paul was so shocked at how we were living that he sat us down and tried to talk some sense into us.

The other thing that got me down was shortage of money. Some of the French riders got a small monthly wage, but all we got was free accommodation. And, unlike in Belgium, all prize money in France is paid to the club at the end of the season, when it is divided up between the riders. I had no afternoon job, and when my money ran out I started borrowing. By the start of the next year I had amassed sufficient debt for it to take the whole of my first pro year to pay it off, and I still owe a debt of gratitude to the people who believed in me enough to lend me the money – Monsieur Wiegand, Peter Brotherton and Gerald George.

All in all, I was pretty down in Paris. I wish I could have been more like Pete Longbottom; he drank in the atmosphere and loved French life. Pete enjoyed the whole experience while all I did was bitch about things, which in the end only made me even more unhappy.

In recent years I have regretted letting a lot of my life pass by without really appreciating it, because I was always getting lost in what was wrong with it. It was first brought home to me towards the end of my cycling career, one day when I was out training with Eddy Planckaert. I had just got a new bike from Koga Mijata who were the bike sponsors of my new team, Tulip Computers. It was a nice bike, but I was moaning to Eddy about its colour. Eddy just looked at me, and when I'd finished griping he asked me when I was ever going to be content with my life and what I'd got.

That was a wake up call, another signpost if you like. Pete Longbottom had what I needed to learn. If I think about him I can still feel his radiance, and his enthusiasm for living for the moment he was in. But nowadays I think I'm getting there, trying to use all the lessons I've learned, and trying to live for the moment.

Being with ACBB was also my apprenticeship into the school of hard knocks and double-dealing that is pro cycling. One time we were riding a race called the Franco-Belge, and I had taken the lead after a time trial, which I then defended for a couple of days, surviving some tough climbs and lots of cobbled sections of road.

One of the toughest stages was the day before the final one. We were in Belgium, and towards the finish a rider I had raced with in the junior ranks, Rudy Delouzee, asked me if I wouldn't mind if he could try to win, because the finish was near to his home, and could he count on my support? In return, he promised to help me on the final day. So I said yes, and when he attacked near to the finish, I didn't chase while he rode off to take the victory.

On the final day I suffered a barrage of attacks, but my team managed to keep them under control, just as our team director Claude Escallon had told them to. Then as we came onto the finishing circuit to do several laps and, thinking they'd done what they'd been asked, all the ACBB riders abandoned. I was on my own and the circuit was so small that team cars weren't allowed onto it, either.

Well, you can guess what happened; with two laps to go I punctured. I got a wheel from the bike of a tourist, who was watching by the side of the road, and chased. But while I was chasing, the second- and third-placed riders overall had attacked and gone off the front of the bunch.

As soon as I caught up to the bunch I had to go to the front and chase, with Rudy Delouzee following but refusing to help me because the third placed man was his team-mate. What was worse was that second overall, the other attacker, was Rudy Dhaenens, who I'd been so friendly with as a junior. Of all people I wasn't expecting Rudy to take advantage of my bad luck.

There wasn't time to bring them back and Dhaenens won with Delouzee's team-mate, Jos Haex, taking second overall. I'd been betrayed by someone who I thought was a friend, and by Delouzee, who I'd just done a favour for. No amount of consoling from Claude Escallon could prevent me from grieving about the lost victory that I was sure would have secured a pro contract, and I was determined to pay Rudy back.

Because there were only a few small races in France for amateurs while the Tour de France was on, I went to race in Belgium for a while. One race I did was Ghent–Ypres, where I rode for an English-speaking team that Staf Boone had put together. On the final circuits Dhaenens was away with another rider, and no-one seemed interested in chasing. So I went to the front with just one thought in mind – to bring back Dhaenens – and inch by inch I did it.

Back at the race headquarters Dhaenens' supporters were baying for my blood. Staf Boone was involved with Dhaenens' club, and must have felt like the meat in a sandwich, but I told him to tell Rudy and everyone else it was pay-back for Franco-Belge. That caused a feud between Rudy and me which lasted for years. We both turned professional in 1983 and didn't speak again until 1991.

Rudy was the World Champion by then, but was having a dismal year in the Rainbow Jersey. We were riding the Four Days of Dunkirk when Rudy rode up alongside me and said hello. He was under a lot of pressure with a big contract as world champion, but couldn't produce any kind of results and was looking for a kind word.

It was a funny situation. Looking at him riding alongside me, he was still Rudy, the kid I used to eat chips and mayonnaise with after the disco, the kid who took us to races in his beat-up old Peugeot car. The only difference was our friendship had got lost in our determination to succeed.

A few years after we'd both stopped racing I saw Rudy in the street. I was working, selling hamburgers, and I'd gone for a coffee. Rudy was unloading boxes from the boot of his car, so I asked him what he was doing. He said that he was selling nougat to coffee shops and was making a delivery. We both laughed. It was so funny: he had been a world champion and we had both been pro bike riders, but here we were, just two guys trying to make a buck. We sat on the boot of his car and talked for a while, but neither of us mentioned our feud.

Rudy died in a car crash in 1998. I didn't go to his funeral. At the time I couldn't face going there with the things that had happened between us; I thought it would be hypocritical of me to go. Looking back now I should have spoken to Rudy, had it out in the open between us. Now it is too late.

With Rudy Dhaenens – 1983

Towards the end of the season I had won 14 races, and one day Claude Escallon asked me to write down a list of the pro teams I would like to ride for. At the top I put Peugeot, because Phil Anderson was there. A few days later, while I was in Belgium, an offer came from the Peugeot team for $1,000 US a month. Walter Planckaert still wanted me for Splendor, but I asked advice from his brother Willy, who is the most level-headed of the family, and he said I should go with Peugeot because the contract was for two years. So I did.

One other ACBB rider turned pro that year, a Frenchman called Phillipe Lauraire. He was a good sprinter, who I called 'Fat Legs', and he signed for the Spanish team, Teka. I got on well with Philippe, and over the next few years whenever he raced in Belgium he stayed with me.

My final race in 1982 was the GP de Nations, which was regarded as the world time trial championships for amateurs and professionals, in those days, before the UCI created an official title race. It was held in Cannes, on the French Cote d'Azur, and the ACBB boss, Monsieur Wiegand, invited me and Pete Longbottom to stay with him for the two weeks running up to the race.

Wiegand had been the directeur sportif of the great Jacques Anquetil, the first man to win the Tour de France five times. In the evening Wiegand used to show us photos of Anquetil, taken either during races or at the finish. There were piles of them, but as he showed us each one Wiegand kept saying, 'Don't end up like this'.

Anquetil's face was like that of a concentration camp prisoner, hollow-cheeked with wide-open, sunken eyes. Wiegand was trying to warn us of the dangers that lurked in professional cycling, the dangers of drugs and pushing too hard and too far. It was a world he loved, but it was like he was trying to open our eyes to its pitfalls.

Wiegand was a genius at preparing bike riders for a race. In those two weeks with him I was like a flower just brought along to bloom on the right day. Pete and I rode for a couple of hours together each morning. Then, in the late afternoon when the heat of the day had gone, we went out behind Wiegand's car to get some speed into our legs. He and his wife fed us properly and cared for our needs, but every day I threw away the vitamin pill he gave me. I trusted him, but I wasn't taking any chances after all those photographs he'd shown me. After just one week of this treatment I won a time trial in Grasse by over three minutes. Wiegand was so impressed that he asked Peugeot to up my money a little bit; which they did, a little bit.

The following Saturday I rode the third fastest lap in the 'Nations'. Only Bernard Hinault and Bert Oosterbosch were faster, although as professionals they had to ride two laps, whereas the amateurs only rode one. It didn't matter though, it was still a great ride and I won the amateur event by five minutes over 45 kilometres. In two weeks Monsieur Wiegand had worked wonders with me by creating an environment where I felt nurtured and safe, and where I could perform at my best.

Professional cyclists are constantly looking for super form. They search for a conditioning of the body that takes them to another level of performance, because for most riders they have to be on another level to win a really big race.

Correct training is the biggest factor in finding good form, but there are times when rest is equally important. Then there are emotional factors. I have noticed riders who have fallen in love and risen to another level. A change of training environment can do the same, or an understanding ear from the team director, or even something as simple as a change of shoes: they can all set the big wheel in motion.

Still, super-form can be an elusive thing. Then, either as a response to pressure from outside or the simple desire to succeed, riders are tempted to seek pharmacological help: drugs. And, unfortunately, it is often the easiest way, as it is difficult to programme your body for the first weekend in April, or any other time of the year you need a result.

Monsieur Wiegand did me a big favour during my stay with him, bigger than just getting me ready for a race. He had shown me what was possible with perfect preparation, and with those pictures of Anquetil he tried to show me what can happen if you chose a different way. His lessons and his warnings were to be major influences on me in the years to come.

8

Gerrie Knetteman

It is 3 November, 2004 and I have just received a text message from one of my best friends, the 1984 Olympic cyclist Gary Trowell. It says that an Australian rider we both know, Glen Clarke, has had a stroke.

Yesterday, the 1978 World Professional Road Race Champion, Dutchman Gerrie Knetteman, died from a heart attack. Last year two of my former team-mates with the Tulip Computers team died. Michael Zanoli had a heart attack and Johnny Dauwe hanged himself. For all of them, the rooster had come home.

Gerrie was a really fun guy, the eternal joker. Someone who took life as it came, and was always positive and vibrant. When I turned pro in 1983 Gerrie was still very much a star, and riding for Peter Post's legendary TI-Raleigh team. In the Tour of the Mediterranean, which 'De Knett', as we all called him, had won three times. I was sixth in the final time trial.

'Sixth,' you say. 'What's so good about that?' Well, look at who was in front of me: Knetteman; World Pursuit Champion, Bert Oosterbosch; five-times Tour de France winner, Bernard Hinault; six-times second in the Tour and once a winner, Joop Zoetemelk; and the time trial specialist, Jean-Luc Vandenbroucke. I figured that if you'd just turned pro and they were the only guys who could beat you in a time trial, then you could believe that one day you might win one.

Later that year 'De Knett' gave me some advice that helped me achieve that ambition. We were chatting during the quiet spell of a race, and he told me that whenever I rode a time trial I should ride as if I was riding for the leader's jersey. It didn't matter if I was tired, or if I was last on the classification, I should ride as if it was for victory. He said that if I didn't do that, then on the day I was riding for victory, I would make a mistake that would cost me the race.

He couldn't have been more helpful. He told me how to prepare on the morning of a prologue time trial. How to plan my day so that it all became second nature. How to ride the circuit on the morning and commit it to memory, so that back in my room I could close my eyes and run through the circuit, planning my gear changes and lines through the corners, visualising them so that any possibility of making a mistake was eliminated. In the next two years I won six prologue time trials.

In one of those prologues, at Paris–Nice in 1985, I beat Oosterbosch by one tenth of a second and put riders like Hinault, Sean Kelly, Phil Anderson, Laurent Fignon and Stephen Roche up to 17 seconds behind me. It was 'De Knett's' advice that put the first pieces of the puzzle of doing that into place for me.

But while I am reflecting on Knett's death, I remember that Bert Oosterbosch, too, died in the mid-nineties from a brain haemorrhage.

I rode my first Tour de France in 1984, and I took a hell of a beating. One day in the Alps I was dropped in the neutralised section at the start of the stage. As soon as the neutralisation was over we had to go up the giant Galibier climb. My mate, Paul Sherwen, was the second rider to be dropped, so we rode together up the 38-kilometre ascent.

Near the top we caught Knetteman, who was also struggling. As I rode up alongside him he turned his sweat-streaked face to me and said in that comical way of his, 'I will never be a climber'. Dropped, and with three terrible climbs in front of him, Gerrie was still the joker. From then on whenever Paul Sherwen and I met we would greet each other with, 'Hey, climber'. I hope Gerrie is climbing now.

I have only mentioned a few of my comrades who've fallen; there have been many more. It happens to us all some day, but I can see the sandman and he's coming for me. I feel that I will not be old when I die. In fact on some days I feel like a walking time bomb, like I could go off at any time. What else can I think when I see the men who I knew and worked with dying around me?

It scares me, but also it's OK. I did what I did, and if that has consequences, like it has had for others, adversely affecting their health, their life expectancy, then for me that's OK. If that has consequences for me it's fine. I did what I did. I lived it and I loved it. I have even picked out my place. In fact, I did it years ago.

There is a towpath running alongside the canal between Ninove, the town where the Tour of Flanders finishes, and Geraardsbergen. Along there, between the iron bridge and Zandbergen, the trees overhang the path and the water, and the grass grows long to the water's edge. In summer, ducks glide over the water. In winter, the fields are white with frost. I have ridden along that path a thousand times, and it is there that I want my ashes spread.

With Gary Trowell – 1981, Melbourne Velodrome

9

Zane Peiper

It has been a couple of months since I last wrote anything for this book. I have started a new job as a directeur sportif with a top Belgian team, Davitamon-Lotto, and it has been a hectic time with a lot of new things to learn.

As I write this I am at ten thousand metres, flying first-class back to Europe from Australia, where I was directing the team in the Tour Down Under, one of the first races of the 2005 professional season. Our stay in Australia has been good for the team, with Robbie McEwen winning the Australian road championships and three stages in the TDU.

Success has helped the team bond, so much so that some of the personnel have commented that they've never experienced such togetherness before. Actually, I have to say that I have only had the same feeling once before, and that was with the Panasonic team in 1989, when Eric Vanderaerden won four stages, took the overall and won the points classification in the Nissan Tour of Ireland, and even then it was less than we have now.

But I'm not letting myself get carried away. I have told myself to enjoy this fantastic experience, while not forgetting that the opposite could be just around the corner. It was a wise sage who once said, 'Don't be too happy and don't be too sad'. What he meant was, keep your emotions in check and you won't be thrown around by the ebb and flow of life. As I sit here I am only too aware of that situation, because just a few months ago my life was so completely different.

On the morning of the first day of the team's stay in Australia, as I descended the steps of the Hilton hotel in Adelaide, I looked across at the little park in the middle of the square. In it I could see the bench on which I'd sat eight months before, on a day that was one of the worst in my life.

The weather had changed as Autumn blew in from the south, bringing with it a cold wind. I had just posted a package to my son, and made a call to him that had ended in a bitter conversation with his mother. Access to my bank accounts had been blocked, and I was waiting for my vehicle to be fixed after having an accident in it. I had no job, no home, nothing left to hold on to for safety. I felt totally vulnerable and sat on that park bench wondering what would become of me. Then I was crushed, and now I am directing a ProTour team, my dream job. The two experiences were so opposite that it feels uncanny.

The reason I was on that park bench was that I had separated from my wife, Christina, after 19 years of marriage, and returned to Australia intending to settle there. But first I decided to fulfill a life dream by travelling around the whole continent. Deep down I'd always thought Christina wanted that, too, but she didn't.

I had been in Belgium for nearly eleven years after my pro career had finished. While I was racing I never thought about Australia; I was totally preoccupied with cycling. But when I stopped, there was a void that had been denied for a long time. Unless you have been through the same thing yourself it is hard to explain about homesickness, or even stronger, the magnetism the place of your birth exerts on you. I often wonder how the immigrants felt who left their own countries to start new lives, and had no hope of going back.

I had eleven years of waking to the grey skies of Flanders, and thoughts of Australia were with me from morning to night. At first, I could deal with it: I got on with my life working in the catering and fast food business with my wife. We built the business up 300% over the decade after I stopped racing but, as many couples do, we lost track of each other over time. So, for a hundred different reasons, I decided during 2003 that I'd had enough.

Christina and I had had a child in 1998, a boy we called Zane after the famous American writer, Zane Grey. I had waited all my adult life for a child, and I felt the moment he was conceived. The morning after I got up and went into my meditation room, got down on my knees and prayed. 'Please Lord, let it be so', and it was. Zane Peiper was born at 11.30 pm on 26th April, my birthday, a gift of unparalleled importance.

Christina was in labour for 24 hours, and fought a battle that makes the pain and suffering I went through in the Tour de France pale into insignificance. At 11 o'clock I went into the hallway of our house and sunk onto the floor, a mess of emotions. I know it can't happen nowadays, but I was afraid I was going to lose them both. When Zane finally popped out, I held him and the first thing I saw were his thighs. He had bike-rider's thighs, and I hadn't even looked to see if he was a boy or a girl yet. Christina and I had met on my birthday, so 26th April will bond the three of us forever.

With my relationship with Christina ended, there was nothing stopping me going back to Australia, but Zane. Many people suggested I stay in Belgium for him, even stay in the relationship for him. But it was like I had no choice: the energy behind the attraction to be in Australia and be Australian again, to feel the land and see the sunset, were more powerful than I was. I knew that if I didn't answer that pull then it could have been the end of me.

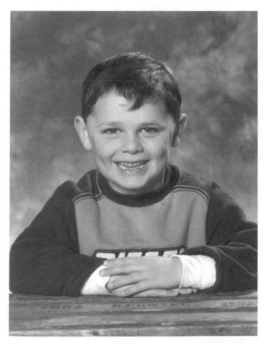

Zane

Leaving Zane behind was the biggest and hardest decision I've ever made in my life. I knew I was going back to Europe at the end of June to work as a guide on the Tour de France for Bike Style Tours and I would see him then, so there was some light at the end of the tunnel. But it didn't really make it any easier.

Once in Australia I bought a Toyota Land Cruiser troop carrier for my trip. It had a top that popped up, so you had two levels, the top one being for sleeping in. There was kitchenette down one side and a bench seat down the other, which you could also make into a bed. It was built for rough travel with double spares of everything: diesel tanks, batteries, and it had a refrigerator, plus a 50-litre water tank slung under the body.

I had mapped out my route years before, doing the south in the summer and the north in the winter, because that is the dry season up in the tropics. I drove 36,000 kilometres in a figure of eight, and I slept on the ground for the whole trip – five months, in a one-man tent called a 'swag', which was just high enough to lay your body flat with a little space around the head.

I travelled through deserts, over rivers, saw wild animals and even had some of them come into the vehicle. One night, while I was sleeping in the swag, a snake slithered over the top of it. I'd heard stories of snakes slipping into the sleeping bags of stockmen out in the bush on cold mornings, so from then on the zips on the swag were done right up.

On another night I was sleeping in my truck with the rear doors open because of the heat. Then in the middle of the night I was woken up by the sound of scratching coming from inside the truck. I sat up in my sleeping bag and was confronted with an enormous possum, an animal the size of a big cat, climbing into my bed. I screamed at it and it fled, but it was another lesson for me.

My trip around Australia was a healing and a cleansing experience, but also one of extreme heart searching. There were times of extreme joy, and times of utter misery at missing my son. Then there were times when I sat sweating with fear at what the future held for me, and where I would end up. What would I do for work? Where would I live? And could I ever find love again? To see fathers with their sons in the shower blocks of camping areas was so painful, and many nights I woke up in tears after a dream about Zane.

Still, for all that, the trip gave me a peace that had been missing before. Twice I felt like I was at home for the first time in my life. The first time I was travelling east to west along the famous Gun Barrel highway through the Great Western Desert, 1,150 kilometres of dirt road with only three filling stations, and they only sold diesel. No towns, no houses. The second time was in the Kakadu National Park, an Aboriginal area of utter beauty in the Northern Territory.

Growing up in the East, I had never seen Aboriginals, their numbers having been decimated there in various ways long before I was born. My grandfather, who had been shearing sheep all over Australia, told me about them and his love for the 'Black fellows,' as he called them. He thought that they were the only men you could trust, so long as they were away from alcohol. Along the Gun Barrel there is no petrol for sale because there is a ban on alcohol in the Aboriginal areas, so they try to sniff petrol, the shortest way to kill your brain.

In the last 30 years political correctness has changed much in Australia, but racial discrimination has changed much more. Fifty years ago, when my grandfather was shearing sheep, there were only black fellows and white fellows. Later on you could only say 'Aboriginals'. Now you can only say 'indigenous people', but whatever you call them they've still been removed from the streets of the east where tourists might see them.

We might not like it, but injustice is part of human nature, and like so many other races around the world the Aboriginals have been to the extremes of persecution. Not all of it was premeditated. The early settlers were mostly newly released convicts from the lowest classes in the Commonwealth, who really didn't want to be in Australia but didn't have the choice. The Aboriginal tribes had lived for thousands of years, exactly in harmony with nature and with each other, but when the white man arrived, with his sicknesses and his greed, their lives were changed forever.

Now the Aboriginals are all in reservations, receiving their monthly pay-cheque from the government to stay there, but they live in a no-man's land, distanced from their old ways. No longer do they have to hunt and gather like the nomads they were, but now they live in houses and drink alcohol to replace their holy corroborree. They can't work because they do not value material things, so they live in neither world – not ours and not theirs.

At the end of the Gun Barrel I stopped at a town called Laverton, and as I walked down the main street I passed three Aboriginal girls, all about 12 or 13. After I passed, one of them yelled out to me, 'Hey, white fella.' I turned round and she gave me the biggest smile you could imagine, you should have seen those white teeth glimmering in her beautiful black face. That is the Australia I came back for.

Another time while driving on the North–South Highway towards Alice Springs, I saw four cars up ahead on the side of the road with lots of people getting out of them. At first I thought there had been an accident, but as I drew level I saw that they were Aboriginals climbing out of the cars through the spaces where the windows had been, and running off into the bush with their dogs following after them. Later at a fuel station, the white guy who owned it had an Aboriginal wife, and she told me that they smashed the windows of their cars so that the dogs could get out quickly to go hunting. It was just another thing that proves we don't understand them, and they don't understand us.

In the last weeks of my travels I found myself in the centre of Australia again, just out from Alice Springs at a place called King's Canyon, where it had been raining for three days, something that rarely happens in the desert. I was at a low point, trying to find some meaning in my life to hang on to. I asked myself what it was that I wanted. Then all of a sudden the answer became clear: Zane my son, he was my priority. I had to be close to him.

I spoke to Christina on the phone and asked her if she was willing to give it another try. What she said stopped me in my tracks. She said that she never wanted to be with a person like me again in her life. I still don't really know what she meant, but I think it was because she thought that other women were after me, which had always been a problem between us. She never liked me having a life outside of her life.

A bike rider in Belgium does attract a fair bit of interest from the opposite sex, but since I'd stopped racing Christina slowly began to begrudge me going out on my bike. Even if it was two hours twice a week, just to keep some sanity, if I stopped for a coffee and was 20 minutes late she would sometimes go mad. I wasn't seeing anybody, but she would accuse me of doing that. Sometimes I wanted to take an axe to my bike and chop it up and say, 'There, are you happy now? You've taken my last thing away'.

I think now that I can see things from her side. She saw her father leave for another woman, which ripped the family apart. A fear of losing me seemed to take her over, and as long as she had me at home, or we were working together, she had control. But once we began to drift apart, she didn't have that and she couldn't live with it. Now, I know we can't both be right. She believes what she does, but so do I.

So that I could stay a part of Zane's life I needed a place of my own where he could come and stay. I also needed a car to get me around, and to get those things I needed a job. I had done a First Aid course in Australia and applied for a flight steward's job with Quantas, but had received no reply. The job would have suited me: I could travel, which I love, and I would have been able to see my son when I flew in and out of Europe, but I still would have been able to live in Australia, which is what I had thought I wanted.

However, during the months I'd been on my own, I had realized that being a part-time dad wasn't an option. History had repeated itself: my mother had been away while I was young and now I had put my child through the same pain. It had to stop.

I left Australia for Europe towards the end of June 2004 and spent two weeks in Belgium close to my son, before going to the Tour de France to do some work as a guide for my friends at Bike Style Tours. I had decided at King's Canyon that I wanted to be involved in cycling again; it was what my heart told me I wanted to do, and being alone for the first time in a long time I could finally hear what it said. So while I was on the Tour I asked all the people I still knew in the bike game for a job.

I was prepared to do anything – wash cars, carry suitcases, any job was fine. Then during the last week of the Tour I saw Eddy Merckx coming out of a restaurant in Grenoble. I went over to him and complimented him on how well he looked, now that he'd lost some weight, and saw he was with Henrick Redant, one of the directeur sportifs with the Lotto-Domo team. I had raced with Henrick and knew him well, so I asked him if there was any chance of a job with Lotto. He said he would see what he could do and asked me what sort of position I was looking for. Then to my surprise he suggested directeur sportif or public relations. I didn't say a word. If he could suggest those positions, he could see I was capable of doing them, and so the ball had started to roll.

By the end of the Tour I had two or three possibilities for jobs, but didn't want to get my hopes up too high. I tried to push things along by making some phone calls. One of these was to Robbie McEwen, a fellow Australian who raced for Lotto and had just taken the Green Jersey in the Tour for a second time, asking him to put in a good word for me.

But, by the end of September, I was beginning to give up hope. I especially wanted the job with Lotto, but knew I was up against stiff opposition from other candidates who had more experience and who were already working in cycling, whereas I had been out of it for nearly 12 years.

Then, one evening in October, I got a phone call from Marc Sergeant, the manager of Lotto, and a man I had raced with in the Panasonic team, telling me I had got the job. It was one of the peak moments of my life. I couldn't believe my luck, and believe me Lady Luck had played a big part in it. Even though there were four Australians in the team, and I had raced, trained, and been in the same team with all the other directors and the manager, still the lack of experience had worried me.

We have spent the Winter preparing for the 2005 season, the first of the new ProTour, with a team that has been re-built from the ground up. I now have an apartment two kilometres away from my son, and the team will give me a car. Life can be so sweet.

10

Robbie McEwen

I really admire sprinters. I worked for some of the best when I was racing and studied them up close. Sprinters really understand what responsibility is: they carry it on their shoulders every time they have the team working for them. They ask riders to close gaps, to pull all day, even to take risks. And then on any given day there might be five or six sprinters from different teams asking the same, but only one can make his team happy. Second place is nowhere, and you're left at dinner with a lot of frosty looks if not outright bad feeling. No wonder some of them get a bit cranky.

Somehow, without even knowing him, although we only lived 20 kilometres apart, I became a fan of Robbie McEwen. I read about him, heard people talk, and felt he was a lot like Eric Vanderaerden. If Eric asked you to ride for him, he tried with everything he had to deliver, and most of the time he did deliver. Robbie is like that, and like Eric he is the sort of sprinter I would have ridden for with my heart as well as with my legs.

After the World Championships in Zolder, Belgium, where he was beaten by the sprint master Mario Cipollini, I saw how disappointed Robbie was on the podium. I sent him a text, recalling my own disappointment in the Worlds at Ronse in 1988, after I missed a medal in the final metres, and told him to savour the moment of the good ride he'd done, not spoil it by dwelling on what might have been, like I had. He texted back that he understood.

My mother had come to Belgium and stayed with me during the Tour de France that year, when Robbie was winning his first Green Jersey. A few days after the Tour finished we had been watching the end of a stage of the Tour de la Région Wallone, which finished in Flobeq and we had to drive past Robbie's house to get home. Outside there was a mass of cars in the street, some sort of celebration going on, and my son Zane asked if we could go in and see Robbie. I thought for a moment and said we'd go and see him one day when he wasn't going so well, because then he'd maybe need our support. That is how I see my relationship with Robbie still.

After last year's Tour, and Robbie's second Green Jersey, I had returned to Europe to be close to my son, after being away in Australia. I had no job and no place of my own, just like the first time I came to Belgium 27 years before. I rang Robbie and asked if he could put in a good word for me regarding the opening as a director at Davitamon-Lotto. Robbie had a lot to do with me getting that job. There were four Aussies in the team, which counted for me as well, but it was Robbie who was there for me.

We aren't what you call good friends, though, and in light of our two roles within the team that is good. I am still a fan, but I can't let that mean I do more for him than anyone else. In fact, I probably do less because I realise that Robbie has enough people around him who want to help out a champion.

Former Italian World Champion Giuseppe Saronni once said that Mario Cipollini was the smartest rider he ever saw, because Mario never did more than he had to. He knew exactly where he could win and he did just that, nothing else. Robbie is like that: he knows where he can win; he knows his opponents and the best way to beat them; and he knows how to dose his energy throughout the season so he can win consistently from January to October. In these days of specializing there aren't many riders who have the drive to do that, especially after ten years, like Robbie has.

Eric Zabel has been an example of professionalism over the last 15 years. A man who has ridden with his heart from early season until October, and Robbie is following in his footsteps. To have a rider like him in a team is a luxury, because Robbie McEwen needs to win, and win often. He is never content, but he also knows when enough is enough. Motivation and control are two of a directors' responsibilities, but with Robbie they come as part of the package.

Many riders think he doesn't train hard enough, because they never see him out riding. But, as Marc Sergeant was at pains to point out when I first joined the team, Robbie knows his body perfectly and how to get it into the right condition at the right time.

He has a circuit he uses to do his sprint training on, quite near to his house. It is five kilometres around, and each lap he does a 300-metre nearly standing-start sprint in the 11 sprocket. Sometimes he does as many as ten laps. Also, when he is home from the races, he gets into the gymnasium and does upper body work. Have you seen the muscles in his arms? There isn't a rider like him in the bunch.

I have worked with Robbie now for six months. I've had time to see how he ticks, and now I've discovered his angry mode. That is how he is when he's focused, angry, or at least it seems like anger. Nearly every time I've seen him in that mode, we've been on a winner. He is so focused that even if you were standing in front of him he would not see you, and yet, after the race he is a different person, the Robbie who just likes a laugh and a joke.

All in all he's a fairly uncomplicated individual. Let him prepare in his own way, steer clear when he is in angry mode and everything will be fine. But even Robbie's evenness and professionalism can be thrown, and that is one thing he shares with most other pro bike riders.

The morning after his first stage win at this year's Tour of Italy, Robbie came to the breakfast table and found there was none of his favourite 'Crunchy Muesli' cereal left. Immediately he got angry and stormed out of the room towards the truck where we keep all our supplies, with me in tow. I wasn't following to help him find some, because I knew we had none left. I was there to try and calm him down when he found out.

He climbed the steps into the truck, went to the kitchen and started to rummage through all the cupboards. I asked him what he was looking for, even though I knew. Mistake. He was seething, and asked if it was too much to ask of the masseurs to bring along enough of 'his' Muesli for the whole race. I tried to calm him down, and told him we would do our best to get some more.

'Crunchy Muesli' is sold by only one supermarket chain, a Belgian one that only has branches in Belgium, and we were in Italy, 2000 kilometres away. But I'd promised, and I'd promised because I knew how important it was. It was something way beyond tasting better than the other breakfast cereals, at least for Robbie it was.

Sometimes, small things are the only things that keep riders going when they are on a Grand Tour, because every day they are faced with the same thing – tiredness, the same food, the same routine, and a daily dose of pain and suffering thrown in. A call to the kids in the evening, an understanding ear from their partner, music, their computer, books or 'Crunch Muesli' are the only things these guys have to hang on to that are their own. They are the only things that keep them sane and focussed, and often the only thing between carrying on or abandoning the race. I had to get some more 'Crunchy Muesli'.

On the way to the start I rang Marc Sergeant in Belgium. He was travelling to the race in a couple of days, so I told him about the problem. He understood straight away. Air freighting was going to be too expensive, so we decided he would bring three boxes in his luggage, and the wife of a masseur could bring three in hers. And, in the meantime, I had to look for the closest equivalent. Our doctor rang all his colleagues in the other teams, and eventually the doctor from CSC came through with something they had that was nearly the same. Heaven and earth had been moved for 'Crunchy Muesli'.

In the next few days Robbie pulled in another two stage wins. Popeye had his spinach, and I'd seen the importance once more of the little things. From the outside you see the man on the podium, the one who crosses the line first. But behind the giant killer is a normal guy, just as vulnerable as you or I; perhaps more so, because at times those giants really do take some killing.

*Team time trial, Tour de France, 1984. Sean and I
rode 90 per-cent on the front. We finished 4th.*

*Isle of Wight Classic, 1985. Sean and I are on the front, with
Ferdi Van Den Haute, Graham Jones and Paul Sherwen.*

In the Paris–Nice prologue, early in my pro career. I thought,
'If I can finish in the top 10 now, then one day maybe I can win.'

Tour de France, 1987, at the start of one of the big climbs.

In one of the 'Scottish Provincial Criterium' races, 1992.

11

Merckx, Simpson and Thévenet

I spent a quiet winter back in Australia before my first year as a pro. I fasted once a week, I didn't train too hard, and was fresh and ready for 1983 and the professional peloton. My first experiences with the Peugeot team were at our training camp in the South of France. It was a 14-man squad with four other English-speakers in it. I was only looking at a poster the other day; there was Anderson, me, Robert Millar, Stephen Roche and Sean Yates.

That caused a bit of a rift in the team for a start. Some of the French guys were OK, but Gilbert Duclos-Lasalle couldn't handle it at all. There were complaints in the rest of the peloton, too. I was riding the GP d'Antibes, I think it was, and Michel Laurent was complaining about foreign riders. 'There used to be one or two of you, but now you're coming in droves,' he grumbled.

I wonder what Michel would say now? There are twenty Australians in the big teams, never mind any other nationalities. I think that there were only ten English-speakers in the whole of European pro racing when I started. The French, though, were very protective of their own little world. I can remember Duclos telling me off for speaking English: 'This is a French team, you must speak French; not only to us but when you speak to each other, so that we all know what you are talking about.' Actually, I could see the sense in him saying that; we were supposed to be a team after all.

Not that it worked both ways: the French wanted us to integrate, but some of them kept things back for themselves. There was a divide, even if it didn't really affect me because I wasn't competition to anybody in the team at that time.

I enjoyed my Peugeot experience – they were a great team. I didn't know much about the history when I got there, about Merckx, Simpson and Thévenet. It was the organisation that impressed me. Our bikes were ready when we needed them and I got suitcases full of clothes. I must have had 30 tops and 30 pairs of shorts. I was giving them away to all my mates, yet I still had plenty for myself.

The directeur sportif was Roland Berland, and the second directeur was Roger Legeay, who had stopped racing at the end of the previous year. Roger is still a directeur with Crédit Agricole now, and when I saw him in Australia earlier this year he had the same two soigneurs that were on the Peugeot team when I started – Michel, a Belgian from Charleroi, and Francis from Bordeaux. That is what the continuity is like in pro teams: the riders change for money, but the staff tend to stay. Seeing them also reminded me that Phil Anderson always got his massage from Michel, because he said Francis' thumbs always got too close to his arse.

One of the first races I rode was the Tour of the Mediterranean, where I finished sixth in the overall classification. On one stage I got in a break with Bernard Hinault, and that was awesome. We weren't away long, but it was mind blowing. I had so much respect for the guys like him. I rode Milan–San Remo that year as well, and Giuseppe Saronni was there in his Rainbow Jersey. I followed him for 100 kilometres. I just sat in his wheel, totally mesmerised.

My start at Peugeot went quite well, but it was an eye-opener. Nothing in amateur racing prepares you for how hard life is as a pro. After that Milan–San Remo, which I finished all 300 kilometres of, we had to get on a light aircraft and fly to somewhere in France. We got to our hotel at about one in the morning, had a light meal and went to bed. Then we got up at 9 o'clock to do another 250-kilometres race the next day.

I shared the hotel room after Milan–San Remo with Sean Yates, who was a bit overweight in those days. They used to call him the 'Peugeot Poggio Pig'. I was so tired, so spaced, that when I got up in the night to go to the toilet I couldn't find the light switch, I couldn't find the bathroom, but I found the door to the corridor, so I just pissed up against the wall in the corridor and fell back into bed again.

It was a hard programme for a new pro and a lot of that year is lost in tiredness. Some things stuck in my mind. For example, I remember riding the Tour of Flanders and I was in the second group when we were going over the cobbles in Zottegem, and a group of people called out that we were lazy. I thought, what are they talking about? We were in the top twenty, and in those days 250 riders started in Flanders, and they were calling us lazy.

I rode a couple of times in America that year. We did one race called the Tour of the Americas. It was in New York and then down the East Coast. We went back a couple of months later and did the USPRO Championships. The prize money was really good in that race: $20,000 for first place, $15,000 for second and $10,000 for third. Thirteen Europeans went over to America for it, and Paul Sherwen suggested that we form a European combine and put all the prize money we won into a pot to share. We all agreed, except for Eric Vanderaerden, who thought he was going to win the first prize on his own.

Anyway, in the race four of us got away: Davis Phinney, Ferdi Van den Haute, Steve Bauer and me. At the finish Phinney won from Bauer, an American from a Canadian, with Van den Haute third and me fourth. Eddy Merckx was there watching, and afterwards he came over to me and Van den Haute and asked us how we'd let these two amateurs beat us. He was very upset, but two years later when the Americans came over in force, he saw how good Phinney and Bauer were. It was just another example of how the Europeans thought they were the centre of cycling, the only ones who knew how to do anything.

We weren't too bothered about what Eddy had said anyway, because we'd won about $26,000 prize money, but there's a story to that money. We'd arranged for Jonathan Boyer, an American who raced in Europe, to do the 'chop', divide up the money. But a couple of months later I'd had nothing, so I rang Jonathan up and asked him what had happened to the money.

He said, 'It's coming, but there's a bit of a story to it. Your mate Ferdi Van den Haute got hold of the cheques and tried to cash them. Then he rang me and told me they'd been lost, but the bank where they were issued in Canada wouldn't clear them.' That's the thing about being a pro, you have to be so careful. Ferdi was just going to keep that money. So as well as improving as an athlete, you have to become very street-wise and switched on, too.

When I turned pro I didn't realise any of what my job entailed, and I can see a lot of that with new pros I work with now: they don't know the whole framework of their jobs. They don't know how to train to reach a peak, when to back off, when to see the doctor. Then there is all the stuff with money going on around the racing. In that way I was lucky that I had a two-year contract with Peugeot, because you need the first year to learn your job, then your career can start from there.

It's so easy to make basic mistakes. Last week I was the Davitamon-Lotto directeur in the Ruta del Sol in Spain, and Johan Van Summeren was second overall after the second day. Then on the third day he missed the break: 32 men just rode away from 110 starters and Johan missed it.

He was very upset, but I told to him that in the first year you are always going to make mistakes. When I was a first year pro, I was on the start ramp for the prologue of the Tour de l'Aude; everything was ready, I was warmed up, focused, my chain was on the 15 sprocket, the one I used for starts. Perfect, except that, without me realising, my chain was on the 42 ring, the one you use for going uphill, and the start ramp is downhill.

I thought I had paid attention, but I hadn't paid attention to everything, which an experienced pro learns to do as second nature. So instead of starting on the 53x15, I was starting on 42x15, and the prologue was only 2.5 kilometres long. By the time I got going, realized my mistake and sat down, changed onto the 53 and got up to speed again, I'd lost at least five seconds. And I lost the prologue by one tenth of a second to Jean-Luc Vandenbroucke.

I told that story to Vansummeren and said, 'Look, I made a stupid mistake, but I never ever made it again. Now, you're never going to let 32 riders ride away from you again when you are riding for the overall. It is your responsibility to be there, not just the directeurs to tell you what is happening. Also it's no good expecting your team to bridge the gap for you, either.'

But the directeurs also have to realise that these are still young men they are dealing with; they have to learn, but they have to live a little, too. At the end of my first year, down at the Tour of Lombardy, Berland took me aside and said, 'You know the problem with you Allan? I think you've got too many girlfriends!'

All the same, what I learned in my first year set me up for the future. I thought I had been looking after myself, and turned up at the first Peugeot training camp with my garlic pills and wheat germ capsules, but the first thing I learned was how to use a needle. Not for doping, but for vitamin injections, because if you need vitamins it is more effective to inject them.

The whole thing was treated as a sort of initiation rite. Everyone would be in the soigneur's room and you had to inject yourself in the backside while they all watched you. And you couldn't throw the needle in, you had to push it in slowly so that you could feel it going through each layer of fibres. The guys would be lying around on beds and sprawled in chairs, laughing at your discomfort.

Now, to people not involved in cycle sport, that might sound a bit frightening, but it was part of your job. Your job was to be in as good a condition as possible, and it was your responsibility to ensure that. Injecting vitamins was part of making sure you were the best you could be. Taking tablets just won't do it because your body is not forced to take up the vitamin; the tablet has to be digested and the digestive system might not even absorb the vitamin. With an injection, especially intravenously, your body has no choice but to absorb it.

I still didn't take it on board at the start. I rode my first Tour de France in 1984 on nothing, no vitamins. I rode on bread and water for the whole way basically, and I think it was probably one of the worst things I could ever have done. It took me months to get over it, because what they know now is that as your blood values fall – iron levels, vitamins, minerals and hormones – the less well your body runs and you damage it.

Medical support is really important, but I think that the outside world thinks that medical support always means drugs, that anything to do with a needle is drugs, but that's not how it is, although I can appreciate that it's difficult for people to understand. For example, sometimes I used to have iron injected intravenously, which I've heard is quite dangerous, but there was such a proven practice of doing it going on in cycling that it was accepted, and you could feel the effects immediately. Now that practice, and the mindset of allowing it to be done to yourself, might be hard to accept from someone outside of pro cycling.

Of course, I'm not trying to say there were no drugs in cycling; I'm not blind. Right from my first year I heard guys discussing taking amphetamines, although I didn't get involved with it. To be honest, I saw the whole thing as a joke. To me the guys were like kids in the playground; you weren't allowed to have lollies at school, but you had them in your pocket anyway and ate them when the teacher wasn't looking.

The situation had arisen because amphetamines had been used in cycling for ages, accepted and uncontrolled. Then came an age when for several reasons they had to be controlled, but how did you get that mentality of free use out of the riders? It's like allowing your kids to watch TV from the moment they come home from school to the moment they go to bed, then all of a sudden saying you're not allowed to watch TV any more. They are going to kick up, and they are going to keep trying to watch it.

That is what the atmosphere was like when I turned pro. There were controls at some races, but not at others and the guys all knew where and when they were. They would be in the changing rooms like naughty schoolboys, talking about a race in France next week, a 'Chaudiere' race. Chaudiere is the French word for a heater, meaning these were hot races, where you could get a charge and use amphetamines.

I'm comparing the guys to schoolboys, because it is the only way I can get across how drugs were viewed, but of course the consequences of taking drugs weren't the same as the consequences of a schoolboy prank. A lot of lives got messed up by amphetamines. I was speaking to a guy recently who I raced with at Peugeot and we went through the whole team, and some of the guys there had had their lives wrecked by amphetamines. There were even guys I raced with who ended up in psychiatric hospitals because their addiction got out of control. That's the danger, and it's an unseen danger; it might have seemed a joke back then in the eighties, but it is a dangerous joke. Or was a dangerous joke; it's not any more because amphetamines are out of place in this era, but they were the stage setter for what has happened recently.

But at the time I really didn't take the drugs seriously. It went on, but it was outside of my reality to get involved. I got on with racing to my best, and if I got beaten by a guy who charged up then I thought; hey, it's his choice. I was free to have done the same, but I didn't.

People talk about the pressure to take drugs, but I didn't feel any. There were incidents, though. I remember on the last stage of Four Days of Dunkirk – and on the last day in stage races there were never any dope controls when I started – I was having a piss in the bushes and a load of other guys, older pros, were there laughing and joking. I said to them, 'Well, at least you guys are happy today,' and one of them said, 'Look, when you've been a pro as long as us, you will be like this as well.'

I can only remember one comment that was directly aimed at me. It was the night before Paris–Roubaix and we were having a team meeting, talking about everybody's function during the race – who would give up wheels, and who was going to wait to pace one of the leaders back if they had a puncture – and the directeur said about one of the other domestiques; 'Ah, here's my rider, he'll be there in the finale with the leaders. But Allan? He won't be there at all with his aspros.'

That was the only time anybody said anything to me, but it didn't affect me because I thought, if I take amphetamines and get caught in the doping control at Paris–Roubaix I'll be the one to take the fall. The directeur was laughing at me, but it didn't make any difference, and the funny thing was that the guy he was praising got caught the next year, in another team, and got kicked out of the team and it ended his career. I couldn't understand why anyone would take amphetamines to help somebody else. Christ, if you are going to do it, do it for yourself. But that was how it was.

12

Sean Yates

We hit it off straightaway, Sean Yates and me. I went to that first training camp with Peugeot and he was there, already doing some of the same things I did, eating salads and stuff like that. The French thought we were weird eating whole plates full of salads. Eventually the hotel used to just leave the vegetables on the table for us to grate into a bowl.

So we already had a rapport and we started sharing a room. We spent a lot of time together, especially in my second year as a pro when I rode the Tour de France. I think it was quite a special time for us both.

We were the same age, both born in 1960, so we had a lot in common – clothes, music and our outlook on life. We were into 'The Jam', 'Tears for Fears' and some heavy metal bands. Sean was big into 'The Jam'; he used to go and watch Paul Weller whenever he could. And he used to talk all the time about his time trialling back in England, on the Q10/19. 'I'm going home to ride the Q10/19; I'm going to get the record,' he'd say. We used to take the Mickey out of him for getting excited about going and riding these 10- and 25-mile time trials, and being totally motivated for them. It was so funny.

Sean used to do them with his dad helping him; it was something they'd done together since Sean was a kid. One time Sean came back and told me that he was riding this time trial and he punctured, and his dad, Roger, got out of the car and changed his back wheel, then jumped back in the car and left Sean's good back wheel, his special one, in the road. Sean was bloody fuming about it.

My second pro year was different – I had the framework down. I spent my usual winter in Australia and came out a lot stronger. That happens a lot with new pros: if they rest well in the winter they come out a lot stronger in their second year.

I started the racing season with very few kilometres in my legs, but what I had done was really intense – sprinting, riding in small gears, and riding in the sun, of course. My first race of 1984 was in Besseges and I won the prologue; I beat Oosterbosch. Then I went to the Tour of the Mediterranean and Oosterbosch did me in the prologue. So it started really well that second year, and Sean was up there in all those prologues as well.

Sean had turned pro the year before me, but I sensed that because I was so driven I inspired him to do more. In those days he was in my wheel, whereas in reality he was a much better bike rider than me. He had far more capacity and far more strength. Whereas all I had was guts and courage, and the will to succeed. We were together so much, they used to call us the Siamese twins.

Phil Anderson, who was still with Peugeot when I started in 1983, was quite stand-offish with Sean and me. I really looked up to Phil; he was so dedicated to his job. He changed much of what cycling was, much of the old Euro pro ethic, through his strength of character and professionalism. I can remember being so proud and so emotional when I crossed the line in the 1983 Amstel Gold and saw him on the podium after winning his first Classic. I had trained with Phil in Belgium the week before, a five hour ride, constantly on the 53x15 on the flat and Phil tearing me apart on the hills. He was just awesome, strong as an ox, and after four hours I was gone.

But Phil thought Sean and I were just two kids who didn't know a thing, just messing about riding our bikes and having a laugh. I remember him doing this fantastic ride to hold everyone off on his own in the Tour de l'Aude in 1983. The whole peloton, apart from us Peugeots, were chasing, but Phil's lead was going out – 30 seconds, one minute, two minutes, and we were just hanging on at the back. It was amazing, we were flat out and on the rivet just hanging on to the chasers, but Phil was going away.

Well, we saw Phil later in our hotel, and we complimented him on the great ride he'd done, but he just looked at me and Sean with a sort of 'Yeah, whatever' superior look on his face, mumbled something and walked away. We didn't matter, you see, just a couple of kids playing around. And I suppose we were, compared to him. Phil was always thinking about his job, and we would be there listening to music. Sean always had his tapes with him: The Jam, Tears for Fears and Alison Moyet. It was a whole learning period that year.

In my second year, though, we knew much more about it. I don't know what Sean did with his first year; it was like he skipped a year. Every prologue I rode with him in 1984, he was a couple of places behind me. Then he won the prologue in the Four Days of Dunkirk, and I think that stimulated him to greater things. We seemed to feed off each other but later, when his back was against the wall, Sean did even better.

We had a new team doctor at Peugeot in 1984. A high-flying sports doctor, who was going to change the whole team, make us all ride better. After my first race, at Besseges, where I'd won the prologue and finished fifth on the Mont Faron stage, he came to my room one night and told me he was going to give me an injection of this new thing called testosterone, which wasn't on the list of banned substances in those days.

He gave me a 250-milligram injection, then four days later gave me another 100-milligram injection. Now, I remember back in the nineties they used to say a therapeutic dose of testosterone was 5 milligrams, and an Indestor tablet was 40 milligrams, and that was regarded as pretty strong. They used to call those tablets 'brown eggs' or something like that. So I had 350 milligrams in the space of a week, but I was riding really strong. When I got back to Belgium I rode Het Volk, and the weather was terrible. There were 250 starters and I finished last, 27th. Stephen Roche was with me, and he finished 26th. I was so cold I was beside myself.

Whether I injured my knee that day, or the next in Kuurne–Brussels–Kuurne, I don't know, but I was riding in the front group going up the Kwaremont in Kuurne and I just felt the tendon go in the back of my knee, and I couldn't ride. I was off the bike for six weeks, going from one doctor to another. I went from Amsterdam to Brussels, to Paris, looking for someone who could diagnose what had happened and treat it. Eventually I was given the address of someone in Belgium who had worked with football teams, and after three days of seeing him I was back on my bike again, and within three weeks I was racing in the Four Days of Dunkirk.

I was still very naïve, and I thought that this doctor, the Peugeot one, had my best interests at heart, whereas when I think about it now, with the massive dose of testosterone he gave me, he was just touching in the dark; he didn't know what he was doing. I think that dose made me so strong that my own muscles actually tore the tendon. After that episode I got really wary of anybody who was going to have anything to do with treating me medically. I had to know what was going on.

After Dunkirk, where Sean won the prologue and I was eighth, we went to the Tour de l'Oise where I won the prologue and Sean was third, I think, and I went on to win the overall. Then I went to the Dauphiné-Libéré, and I won the prologue there as well. I beat Phil Anderson and Stephen Roche. After that it was the Tour of Sweden and I won the prologue again. I won the time trial and the overall, with Sean third in the time trial and third overall.

With Sean Yates – Tour of Sweden

We were both going really well and got a start in the 1984 Tour de France with Peugeot. Phil Anderson and Stephen Roche had both left the team by then, but with Robert Millar still there, and selected for the Tour, we had three English-speakers starting with five French guys. I think that was a first.

I was third in the Tour prologue behind Hinault and Fignon. It was incredible, having the fastest time all day until those two came in. Then I finished third on the first stage in a bunch sprint, and missed out on the Yellow Jersey by just three seconds because Ludo Peters had been away in a break and won some time bonuses. Next, the Peugeot team finished fourth in the team time trial, with basically just me and Sean riding on the front. It was a really good start and I held the White Jersey for the leading young rider for ten days. Most days I was high up in the bunch sprints, and Sean and I were really motivated, but then it started to get hard.

I've said before that I didn't take any vitamins or anything during that first Tour, and neither did Peugeot have any medical support on the race. The doctor who'd given me the testosterone at the beginning of the season had just disappeared from the scene. After ten days I started paying the price of not being looked after.

Sean and I both finished the Tour really tired, and then we rode the criteriums. So we had ridden the 21 days of the Tour, then 25 criteriums back-to-back. We rode all the post-Tour criteriums in Holland, plus we rode criteriums once a week in England, and we rode some in France. Sometimes we'd ride a criterium in England, fly back here to Belgium and drive to a race in France, then drive back to Holland. And we did that for 25 days straight, still with no medical support. It took me a long time to recover from that.

It was still an incredible experience for us, travelling around together, just two young men. It was hard, but we had so many laughs. My race number during the Tour had been 69, and my name, Peiper, loosely translated in Dutch means a female giving a male oral sex, so you can guess at the cat-calls I got at the races in Holland.

Looking back now and thinking about it, it was an incredibly free time. We had nothing, so there was no fear of losing anything. We were young. We had no one saying do this or do that, like people of our age who were in a normal job had. Provided you turned up at the race, looked good and did your job everything was fine. But it was during those criteriums that I found how easy it was to get carried away and sucked into the climate of pro racing in those days.

We were getting changed for a race in the South of France, and in the changing room there were some older, more experienced riders. They had some amphetamines and a needle, and were passing it around. They had a little bit left over and asked if anybody wanted it. I tried it, put the needle in and rode the 100-kilometre race like it was nothing. I was in heaven.

So that was my first experience of amphetamines, but it left me tired for the whole of the next week and I thought, I can't do that again. The drugs let me go beyond what I was capable of doing, and the race took more out of me than it should have done.

The temptation was still there, though. Next year in a Dutch criterium it had been decided before the race that I had to be in the first break. Well, I knew that one of the riders I got on very well with had a tablet in his back pocket, so I went and told him I had to be in the break and I needed the tablet, which he gave me. A bit later I got it out of the silver paper it was wrapped in, and was just about to swallow it when he came up to me and said to me, 'Give me half.' So I bit it in half, gave him one piece and took the other, but I don't think I felt anything from it that time.

That was the last of my experiences with amphetamines. I know I have an addictive nature, so I knew I had to be very careful. The early eighties was the end of the amphetamine era anyway.

There were a lot of other changes going on in pro cycling at that time, too; 1984 was the really big year of the Panasonic team. All the old guard from the Raleigh squad, which had previously been such a force in cycling, had gone with Jan Raas to his Kwantum-Hallen team, and Peter Post had built a new team with Panasonic.

Eddy Planckaert was with Panasonic, and Phil Anderson had gone there. They were a great team and had a great year in '84. Because of the kind of races I'd won, prologues and time trials, I was told that I'd made a good impression on Peter Post. Also, the Planckaerts had spoken to Post about taking me in the team, and I knew one of the soigneurs with the team, Dirk Nachtergaele. He used to give me advice about what vitamins to take. He used to kill himself laughing at the seaweed capsules and garlic pills I had so much faith in, but he had a soft spot for me, and he spoke to Post about me as well. I really wanted to ride for Post.

During the Tour in 1984 I had already had an offer from another team – Carerra. Their directeur, Davide Boifava, came to me during the Tour and said that I could name my price to ride for him. I asked if he would also take Sean Yates, but he wasn't interested, so I said no.

I had really found a big brother in Sean. Even though he was in my wheel at that time and being motivated by my motivation, I felt really protected by Sean. Being with Sean was like going around with a bodyguard. I felt like he was always keeping me safe, watching my back and looking after my best interests.

I believe everything happens in life as it's meant to but, looking back, it wasn't a good move to stay at Peugeot with Sean, because I didn't do it for the right reasons. If I had gone to Carerra maybe I would have had a different career – not better, but different – because they were a great team. They were taking Roche and they had Guido Bontempi.

At the start of 1985 I won the prologue in Paris–Nice, held the leader's jersey for a few days and lost it on the Ventoux, but I was still seventh to the top and Sean Kelly took over the lead and won the race. I was riding well, even though my motivation was being affected by the attitude of the Peugeot team.

I wanted to ride for a team that raced as a team. At Peugeot we had a good sprinter in Francis Castaing, but I couldn't get the French guys motivated to lead him out. He was French and they were French so why didn't they want to do it? I was constantly banging my head against the wall with them.

I couldn't understand it. They could see what Panasonic were doing – so organised, winning races and winning money. I was trying to get Peugeot to think like Panasonic, but the mentality wasn't there. I think French teams haven't changed much now. They never seem to have any sprinters, and when they have a sprinter they don't have any connected form of teamwork to get him in the right place. They never get on the front and make the tempo to keep things together. They never have a system of lead-out men: one to take the sprinter to the last kilometre; another to take over from there, and so forth.

But also I wonder why the French never seem to produce a top-line sprinter. Jacques Esclassan was good in the seventies, and Castaing was good. Frédéric Moncassin and Jean-Patrick Nazon have popped up now and again, but the French have never produced a really top-line sprinter since Andre Darrigade way back in the fifties and sixties. They haven't had a Cipollini, or a Robbie McEwen, or a Petacchi, or a Tom Steels. Why is that?

I let the Peugeot attitude really wind me up in 1985, and I remember having a big argument with Duclos-Lassalle during the Tour de France. We were staying in this school, in Pau I think it was, and I was getting a massage from Francis, who liked speaking English to me. So there we were chatting away and Duclos comes in, and starts: 'You are in a French team now, you have to speak French.' He went off big time, and so did I. We had a big blow-up about this French speaking thing. I'd gone a year too long with Peugeot.

A few days later the Tour was in Bordeaux and we were staying in the same hotel as Panasonic, so I rang up to Post's room and asked him if I could come and talk to him, and he said, 'Sure'. So I went up to his room, and I was really nervous because I was going to ask for a contract.

I knocked and went in, and Post was sitting there with his second directeur, Jules de Wever. I said that I'd just come to ask if they had a place for me in the team for 1986, and Post asked me how much I wanted to earn. So I said, 'Whatever you think I'm worth'. Jules de Wever said, jokingly; 'What about a jersey and a pair of shorts?' To which I replied, 'Well, if that's what you think I'm worth, then fine'. Then Post said, 'No, don't be silly', and ripped open his Marlborough cigarette packet so that it made a flat piece of paper and wrote down: 'I, Peter Post on this day, hereby sign a contract with Allan Peiper for the seasons 1986 and 1987.' And that was my contract. I didn't get the proper papers to sign until the following January, but with Post his word was his bond.

Sean was very quiet before I went to see Post. We were sharing a room, but things had changed a little between us. I had got married at the start of 1985 and was living with my wife in Blankengberg on the Belgian coast. Sean and I, naturally, were seeing less of each other, and he stopped a lot of the time with Paul Sherwen just over the border in France. He was also quite friendly with another Peugeot rider, the Norwegian Dag-Otto Lauritzen, and roomed with him on a lot of races.

When I got back to the room after making an agreement with Post I was jumping up and down on the bed like on a trampoline, I was so happy. But Sean was a bit subdued. I think that was a difficult moment for him. From that moment really, what we'd had together had gone.

Sean stopped with Peugeot in 1986. I don't think he had much choice, but it turned out to be a difficult year for him. The old Peugeot team was falling apart by then; it was before Z came along and Greg Lemond. It was his fifth year with the team, and from being the Peugeot Poggio Pig and weighing 84 kilos, he'd got caught up in my motivation and trimmed down, done some good rides, but he'd not found the spark within himself yet.

It was a great move for me to go to Panasonic, but that move sparked off the end of the first phase of Sean's career, and in a way the end of the old Sean Yates. After the 1986 season Peugeot told Sean that they didn't want him any more, and up until December that year he didn't have a contract. So I can imagine there was a lot of fear involved for Sean then, thinking he was going to have to stop racing. Then all of a sudden, out of the blue, came a contract from Fagor, and for whatever reason it was, maybe it was taxation, Sean moved to the South of France.

That was the turning point for him; it was when he changed as a rider, and he found his own inner spark. I can remember visiting him in the flat he had down there and opening up the cupboards in the kitchen, and all that was in there was a packet of coffee, nothing else. Nothing. No salt, no pepper, no foodstuffs at all, just one packet of coffee.

When Sean got down to the South of France he was away from all other influences. He'd had his back against the wall, so he used to get up in the morning and have a cup of coffee, ride down into town and buy two croissants or two cakes, then ride for six hours in the hills. After that, he'd get changed at home, go down to the beach, lay on the beach and sleep or go wind-surfing, then on his way home get a pizza. And that's all he ate, and he went from 83 kilos to 75 kilos; he lost 8 kilos.

He came out in 1987 with some really good results, and in 1988, too. He won stages in Paris–Nice, the Tour of Spain and the Tour of France. In the Midi-Libre he even won a stage in the mountains.

What Sean's change taught me was that if you do what's right for you, you do what's right for everybody. I made the wrong decision for me in 1984 when I turned down Carerra to stay with Sean, but that was the wrong decision for him, too. Then in 1985 I made the right decision for me to go to Panasonic, but in the end that was right for Sean as well. He became his own man, and his career really started from when he took his life in his own hands.

And it was good for me, too. I had depended on Sean. He was my back-stop, he looked out for me, even though he had far more ability than me. Now I had to start looking out for myself.

With Sean and Mum

13

All racing cyclists, everywhere

It's January 2005, and I did a race today, in Wallonia, the French-speaking part of Belgium. It was a run/bike race. They're quite popular in Europe, teams of two use one mountain bike and must keep within ten metres of each other, one riding and one running. You can swap who runs and who rides as many times as you want, but the idea is for the two of you to get to the finish together in the quickest time.

The race was 23 kilometres long, through forest, over muddy trails and on quiet rural roads. Run/bike doesn't have a federation, so the races are quite relaxed, and coupled with the fact that the pace of life and friendliness of the people in Wallonia is what it was like in the rest of the western world about fifty years ago, I really enjoyed it.

I did the race with my friend Philip, who was the Belgian duathlon champion four years ago, and we finished second, just 30 metres behind the winners. It wasn't a world-class event, just a few people getting together for some fun. For a few of us though, it was as serious as the Tour de France.

Phil and I were leading at the top of the first climb through the forest, but twice we were sent the wrong way. This meant that another team caught us four kilometres from the finish, but we were still there for the win, hammering it out with this other pair. Then Phil jumped off the bike and handed it to me at full sprint. I took the bike by its saddle and got my hand on the handlebars before trying to get on it. Just at that moment the bike's front wheel hit a hole, the handlebars turned around and the bike hit the floor with me on top of it. My hand was gashed open and we had lost fifty metres, but we got going again and brought the pair in front back to thirty metres by the finish. At the line my legs had gone and my lungs were about to jump out of my chest. We lost the race, but we had been in a battle. Fought and lost. Given it our best shot.

In normal life you don't get to be in a battle, not a purely physical one, with adrenaline and pain all mixed in. Isn't that why we love to compete? I know some of you will say that it's because of chemicals – endorphins, being released into the blood that makes you feel good after a race. And that may be so, but if you look deep down it is also about the battle. There is something primitive in the fight to succeed.

I am reading a book at the moment about the First World War. It tells of the horrors of the trenches, but it also tells of the bond of battle, of losing touch with reality and creating another world with different values, where being in a brotherhood is the only way to survive.

I miss bike racing. Nothing can ever replace the feeling I had in competition. The feeling of achievement, not necessarily in winning, but in doing your absolute best. I also miss the bond, the brotherhood. In cycling, like in war, men are bonded by their pain and by their suffering. We feel for each other because we know how each other feels.

In my last year of racing as a pro I rode the Tour of Italy. On one stage I got away on my own, just after a points sprint and not long after the start. It was a 240-kilometre stage with the finish on top of the Terminillo pass, a 20-kilometre climb. But as I rode off I wasn't thinking about the last climb, I was just going for it with everything I'd got, to see how long I could last.

Once I had a lead of 12 minutes on the peloton, Miguel Induráin's Banesto team began riding on the front. My directeur, Jose De Cauwer, drove up alongside their team car and asked them why they were riding after me when I was two hours behind on the overall classification. They said they weren't riding after me, they were just making tempo.

It was a blistering hot day, and I won quite a few primes during my 200-kilometre ride to the foot of the Terminillo. I was determined to get there before the rest, and I did, but they were close. I could hear the thud of the blades on the helicopter that hovers above the peloton, relaying the TV pictures into countless homes. It was getting closer and closer, with a phalanx of warriors beneath it, after my blood.

They caught me just as the climb started and, one by one, the different groups passed me by. Finally, the last group caught me – the one with the sprinters in it, big guys who can't climb but have to survive in the mountains so that they can fight out the bunch finishes in the days to come. My legs had gone; it was all I could do to ride with the group.

A few kilometres from the top I cracked completely, and tears began to stream down my face. I didn't think I would be able to ride to the finish – it was all uphill and I was grinding to a halt. The fear of being unable to finish, and the hopelessness of my situation shattered my spirit.

Then there was a hand on my back and a push. Then another, and another. Even Super Mario Cipollini – who always pissed me off on mountain stages by sitting on the back of the group on the flat, then riding at the front on the climbs for the cans of Coke the fans offered – even Mario gave me a push, and a word of encouragement. I made it to the finish, but only because of the pushes from those men, some of them the same ones who, earlier in the day, had chased me with such spite to end my escape.

My race today brought that all back. One guy told me at the finish that when Phil and I competed in these races, the races were different because we fight so hard to win, pushing the other teams to their limit. After the race is over, whether we've won or lost, we are like brothers who have fought together. There is nothing like it.

With Phil Braems – Run/bike, Winter 2005

14

Robert Millar

I always had a soft spot for Robert; he is eccentric. Mr Eccentric. He was a lot like me in the sense of looking after his body. He was very interested in his food, in health food and not eating rubbish. He also had an eye for doing all the little things, the details of looking after yourself. Like he would get two ashtrays in the hotel room and put them under the feet end of the bed, so when he laid down his legs were raised and the blood would run easily to his heart to help his legs recuperate.

I can remember sharing a room with him a few times and coming out of the shower and he'd be laid on the bed with his sleeping mask on, and he wouldn't let you turn the light on, and you couldn't make a noise. Another thing I remember is that he walked everywhere on tip-toe, like he had cycling shoes on, but he did it no matter what he'd got on his feet.

But when Sean and I were around him we could crack that exterior, the odd little person that Robert was. And I can see a correlation in Davitamon-Lotto between Cadel Evans, and Nick Gates, Robbie McEwen and Henk Vogels, because Cadel is pretty eccentric. Not as extreme as Robert Millar was, but Cadel is different from your average bike rider; he thinks differently and acts differently.

I was driving a team car to the start of the Australian Championships recently, and all the Australian riders in Davitamon-Lotto were in it. Robbie had the front window down and Cadel yelled out from the back, 'Can you close that window?' And Gatesy said, 'Oh pull your fucking head in. What do you think you're going to get, a cold? It's 30 degrees outside'. And I looked in the mirror and saw Cadel's face, and he just cracked up. Now that was good, because I thought Gatesy and Vogels were going to be too hard for Cadel. I was a bit wary that they would crack him mentally, but I can see that they are good for him, and they will look after him.

That's how it was with Sean and me, and Rob. We looked after him and we could get through to him.

We went to a race on the Isle of Wight; it might have been 1984 or '85. Peugeot UK took us over and Sean won it. We were catching the plane back to Belgium from Heathrow, and security wanted to do a check on Robert's bags. Well, he got really irate. He was really abusive to the girl who was looking in his bags, and afterwards I said to him; 'Look Rob, if you ever speak to anybody like that again in my presence, I'll fucking knuckle you.' And it must have stuck, because I never heard him go off like that any more.

Robert wasn't naturally like that, not naturally hard or abusive, but he thought he had to act that way. Maybe it was something to do with where he grew up, in Glasgow. He had put it on, and sometimes he didn't know when to take it off. Sometimes in life you have to act hard, but not with everyone, and Robert didn't always understand that.

That first Tour de France I rode was the one in which Robert won the King of the Mountains, so that made it even more special for me. Sean and I did what we could for him after I lost the young rider's jersey. We rode in the wind for him, and on the climbs when the mountains weren't too steep we fetched bottles, and generally looked after him in the bunch. Then afterwards, riding the criteriums with Robert in his mountains jersey was a good time, and it made me feel very proud.

I had a rapport with Robert. It was not like we were friends, because I don't think it's so easy to be friends with Robert Millar. I don't mean that in a bad way, it's just the way it is. But he felt comfortable with me and Sean. I think he felt accepted. I can see that with Cadel; he wants to be accepted. Cadel needs assurance, and he needs to feel he is accepted. As he is in Davitamon-Lotto.

Now, some people reading this who knew Robert in those days will wonder what I'm on about, because sometimes it looked like he went out of his way not to be accepted. But again that was a front he put up – although, I admit, it was a pretty good one. Going out to be different, to be at odds with everyone, was a safety net with Robert, just in case he wasn't accepted. It was a way of protecting himself from getting hurt.

With Robert Millar and Sean Yates

He still used to do some strange things, though. I was just thinking about this the other day when I was driving on the autoroute in France. To get out of paying the tolls, Robert used to have a big pair of bolt cutters in his car. There are gates before the toll booths that are locked with chains, and at the last gate before the toll, and Robert always knew where they were, he would stop his car, cut the chain and drive off the autoroute. Then he'd come back on by the toll booth entry road, get a ticket and only pay for one stop.

He had a system for the airport, too. He'd drive his car into the car park, take a ticket and leave his car there for maybe two weeks. So by the time he came back he'd have a really big bill to pay. What he would do then was get a buggy, and drive the buggy out of the airport building onto the road and into the car park. Then, I don't know how he did it perhaps he had a magnetic pass or something, but he'd get the barrier to lift, get another ticket so it looked like he'd just driven his car in, and use that ticket to get his car out. It would look as though he'd only been in there for ten minutes.

He was always coming up with these schemes to save money. I mean, who would think about having bolt cutters in the boot of their car? We used to take the piss out of him something wicked. I had five years with Robert, three at Peugeot and two at Panasonic. Robert went with me to Panasonic and was there in 1986 and 1987. Then he went to Fagor, the team Sean Yates was in.

There were some fireworks with Robert and Peter Post, though. Peter had this strict idea of what he wanted in his riders. They had to have good manners; they had to look smart. He had a mould he wanted them to fit, and it wasn't just about how good a bike rider they were. He wanted good looking riders, and riders who could ride hard. I can't put my finger on quite what it was, but the nearest I can think of is he wanted riders that he classed as 'gentlemen'. I think Rob rubbed a bit with that.

Having said that, I still think Peter respected him. Robert did some good rides with Panasonic. He nearly won the Tour of Spain. He should have won the Tour of Spain, but there was something that went off with a car in the final mountain stage, where the rider who beat Rob was protected from the wind by the car for part of the course. He also did a good ride in the Giro: he was second overall and he won the mountains jersey there.

The thing about Robert, now that I've written about him and thought about the length of time I was on the same team as him, almost half of my career, is that I never really knew him. We never had a heart to heart conversation. I never went to his house, and he never came to mine.

But friendship is a strange thing in the peloton. You will lay your life on the line for a guy because he's in your team, then next year when he's gone you may never speak to him again, ever. You make very few real, lasting friendships. I have stayed in touch with Maurizio Fondriest – we phone each other at Christmas, and see each other when we can – but that's about it. There is a spirit in the sport, though, but I guess you could call it camaraderie rather than friendship. I suppose it's the same in other walks of life? You share a bond with many people, but how many can say they have a lot of true, close friends?

It was a whole new ball game for me in 1986 with Panasonic. They had so many good riders: Eric Vanderaerden, Eddy Planckaert, Anderson and Millar; Eric Breukink was just coming on the scene, and there was Peter Winnen. Among that lot I fitted straight into my role as a domestique. I didn't focus on prologues any more, like I did at Peugeot. I'd decided I wanted to be a Classics rider; I wanted to win the Tour of Flanders.

I'd probably taken in that goal during my exposure to the Planckaerts when I lived with them – everything there was about the Tour of Flanders and Paris–Roubaix. Eddy told me that even as a schoolboy all he heard from the family was Tour of Flanders and Paris–Roubaix. With all Flemish bike riders those races are a sort of Holy Grail, but with the Planckaerts they were an obsession.

But as I got involved with Panasonic, a team which really rode like a team, I learned something more about myself, and that was that I am a team person. I am a person that can be of service to other people, and a real asset in a team. It's probably to do with wanting to please everyone, to do with my fear of rejection. With Peugeot, winning, and doing the best you could as an individual, got you accepted. That wasn't what Panasonic wanted from me; they had winners. Being a team-man was where I fitted, where I wouldn't be rejected.

I use some of those same qualities that I used as a domestique in my job now. I try to think for the riders, try to do things and arrange things so that their lives will be better. That is very like the work of a good domestique, and it is also what I have been doing all my life in order to be accepted by people. I think it comes from the scar of my mother's rejection when she chose my father over me when I was a teenager, but also from always being the new kid when we moved around the country to live in so many different places while I was growing up. I felt I had to try harder to please everyone, in order to be accepted quicker. I still do.

But the way I am helps me to see over the ego investment of being first, or who is second, third or fourth directeur in the team. It helps me bridge that, and that stops groups forming within the team. It is very important in a big team that the directeurs are in a line, because the riders will try and come between us. In that respect they're like kids; you know – 'Oh I've tried with dad and he said no, so I'll try with mum,' sort of thing. We all have to be in accordance to stop the riders doing that, and I think I can facilitate that.

But the Panasonic days were my first experience of real team-work. Panasonic winning was now what I lived for. I saw a picture in the papers from the Tour of Quatar recently, and Robbie McEwen was winning, but ten places back with his arms in the air was Fred Rodriguez, the team-mate who'd led him out. And I understood what Fred was feeling. Even though I won 35 races as a pro, that feeling of having your hands in the air because your sprinter had won is the most gratifying thing that ever happened to me as a rider. Also, being there for the team time trial win in the Tour de France with Panasonic, like we did in 1990, was an amazing experience. That feeling of being so powerful as a block was the best feeling I ever had.

But in writing about being a team-orientated person I have realised something else about myself; maybe I didn't have enough self-belief to be a winner, and that is why I became a good team-man. I wanted to be part of something, rather than pushing to be at the top; it was a safer way to acceptance. I said I wanted to win the Tour of Flanders, but when I think about it, what I really wanted was to do well in the Tour of Flanders, to be there, to figure, be part of it.

Hendrick Redant, another of Davitamon-Lotto's directeurs, said to me the other day; 'If I had been you, I would have won the Tour of Flanders at least once. Every year you were there in the finale.' I told Hendrick that I didn't have the strength in my body to win, to make the decisive break over the last 30 kilometres. I mean, in 1989, when I was in the break with Edwig Van Hooydonk, he went up the Bosberg in 53x16. How do you do that with 260 kilometres in your legs? He just left the rest of us standing.

I also told Hendrick that for all the strength he had and the ability he had, he didn't win the races he should have done, either. You see, we all have these psychological kinks, or chinks is maybe a better word. Perhaps Van Hooydonk went up the Bosberg in 53 x 16 simply because he believed he could, whereas I didn't. Maybe in the finale of a Classic it is just as much about what is going on in your head, as it is about what is going on in your legs.

Why didn't I believe I could do it? Well, something that crossed my mind the week after the 1987 Milan–San Remo might help to explain that. That was the race I told you about in the chapter on Phil Anderson, where I was in a break and attacked just before the Cipressa and got away with Eric Maechler. Phil chased us, Maechler saw him, and left me to go on and win. And I was caught just before the line.

A couple of days afterwards I was out training and this thought just popped into my head. I thought, 'Phew, lucky I didn't win'. Lucky I didn't win because … because I would have gone from £20,000 to £150,000, and when you get £150,000 basic contract a year it's not a gift; there is £150,000's worth of responsibility attached to it.

Maybe you're thinking Peiper's crazy; he doesn't want the reward for winning a big race. But it's not a reward – the £150,000 is for winning again. You don't get paid that because of what you've done. Now you are expected to win, and if you don't produce victories there's a whole lot of heat comes down on you.

Last week I was at a reception and a lot of our sponsors were there. I was talking to the head of the Belgian lottery and we were talking about Peter Van Petegem, and he asked, 'Is Van Petegem going to be there in the big races this year?' I said, 'Well, he's been sick recently, but he's getting better. I'm sure he'll be there.' And he looked at me sceptically and said, 'Well, I hope so, because a lot of people are counting on it.' So the sponsors put pressure on the managers and the managers put it on the riders, not just in our team, but in every team. It is how all top sport works.

Now, Peter van Petegem is not a rider who would succumb to that. He is mentally very, very strong. He knows where he stands. He likes to drink a beer, and doesn't give a shit what anybody says about it. He knows exactly how to prepare for a big race. He often didn't get any great results just before he won a Classic. But for another rider who is not as mentally strong, it can become a nightmare.

I had some experience of that early on with Peugeot, when between my second and third years my wages went up from £5,000 a year to £20,000 a year, and I was under pressure to get results. I wasn't so good in the Tour of the Med, and that put me under pressure for Paris–Nice and things began to spiral. I quickly saw that when you get a lot more money you get a lot more pressure, and then you could easily look for other ways to do it. Also success feeds your ego and you want more. You look for that gratification again, and then you put pressure on yourself.

As I've said, that thought after Milan–San Remo just popped into my head for a second, even though I have written a lot about it here, but in doing so I have thought back over the years at how many races I lost in the last hundred metres.

There was the Championship of Zurich, a couple of stages in the Tour de France, and I wonder if there wasn't a mental mechanism there, a blockage that holds you back. Is that the difference between being a winner and a team-man? Because some guys always seem to be in the right place at the right time. They win a lot of races in the last 50 metres, where they just don't get caught. They will attack as a bunch sprint is coming up and hang on to win.

They hang on, but for me it seemed to be different. I would attack, get clear, get a good gap, but coming to the finish I'd start thinking, 'This can't be happening. I can't be winning a stage of the Tour.' And when you think that, you don't win. But how do you sort out that chink in your armour?

I actually spent one winter seeing a psychiatrist and doing subliminal tapes, which had messages on them that are received by your brain on a different level to normal communication. And I felt that the tapes helped me as well – during the winter. But then you get back into the bunch, and you get smashed 15 or 20 times. You've got in your head these subliminal tapes giving you all this belief about yourself but, in reality, you're going out every day and getting your doors blown off.

Eddy Merckx once said at the start of a Tour of Flanders, 'There are probably only ten guys at the start of this race who are thinking about winning, and all the others are just riding to get to the finish.' But how do you change yourself into being one of the ones who are thinking about winning, even planning to win, when you have the evidence of your experiences telling you that you can't win? If it's not within the realm of what experience tells you you can do, it is difficult to believe. Maybe if I could have got rid of that blockage I could have won the Tour of Flanders.

The more I think about it, though, I was a team-man; but I was a good one. Being part of a good team was how I got the most out of myself. When I hear people muttering about how some of the riders in Lance Armstrong's team ride so well for him in the mountains, and they mutter and make accusations about how they are able to do that, all I can say is that when you ride for someone else, and you believe in that person, you can ride well above yourself. I did it all the time.

As a domestique you can ride up front and not get tired simply because there is no pressure on you to win, you are not the one that has got to carry the buck and that gives you more strength. The sprinters get really nervous when their team rides hard on the front all day. If you have your team do that, then lead you out in the sprint, working hard and risking their lives, you are under a lot of pressure.

Anyway, 1986 was my first year with Panasonic and I really enjoyed it. Everything was very professional – good bikes, good care – and I slipped into my role as domestique. I was just doing my job, and was determined to do everything I was told. Well, nearly everything.

Walter Planckaert was in his first year as a directeur, and I knew that every year coming up to the Classics, when he was still a rider, he wouldn't sleep with his wife. I can remember asking him once, 'Well, what does she do then?' And he said, 'She can do what she wants; she just has to leave me alone for the Classics.' That was the old mentality. You can say in the sixties and seventies that they were taking amphetamines, but at the same time they weren't sleeping with their wives. They wouldn't have a bath the day before a race. They wouldn't shave. All these old wives tales.

So Walter came up with this idea that we would all stay in a hotel for a month, and we wouldn't be allowed to go home, and we hadn't to have sex with our wives for a month. I thought, 'Oh Christ', but I was up for anything at that time and I was going to give it a go.

So I didn't have sex for a month and we came to our three most important Classics. In the Tour of Flanders I gave my wheel to a team-mate at the top of the Koppenberg. In Ghent–Wevelgem I gave up my wheel along the coast, and in Paris–Roubaix I gave up my wheel twice to team-mates who'd punctured. Four times I gave up my wheel, and I hadn't had sex for a month. After that I thought, no way am I ever going to do that again.

15

Peter Post

Post ruled Panasonic with an iron rod. He had a very powerful character and most of us were frightened of him. He had this thing when we were eating where he would pick someone to sit next to, and if he sat next to you, you were in for it. We used to say that he had picked a victim.

He would sit and ask you questions that there was no right answer to. If your answer was white, the correct one would have been black. If you said black, it would have been white. Then when you'd given the wrong answer, he had you. I don't know why he did it. Maybe he thought it motivated you.

He did it with me once in Tirreno–Adriatico. I had been riding on the front all week, working for Vanderaerden. We came to the last day, a time trial, and I was shattered, so I thought, I'm just going to ride easy today and try to recover for Milan–San Remo, which was only two days away. We were having breakfast before the time trial and Post sat down next to me and said, 'So Allan, are you riding your time trial bike today or your road bike?' Trick question. If you said time trial bike he would say, 'Why are you doing that, don't you know Milan–San Remo is only two days away? Who do you think you are?' Or if you said that you were riding your road bike it would be, 'Why are you not riding your time trial bike, are you tired? You should be fit and strong enough by now to do a good time trial and still be ready for Milan–San Remo, what have you been doing all winter?'

Anyway, I told him the truth. I told him I wasn't riding my time trial bike because I was tired and wanted to recover in time for Milan–San Remo. So off he went: 'What have you been doing all winter? You've been in Australia lying on the beach haven't you?' And he tore strips off me, but then he said something about my wife. She ran a hamburger stand and Post said, 'Anyway, what does your wife do for a job?' At that Fred de Bruyne, the team's PR man came over and stood between us and said, 'Peter, you're out of line,' and Post just shut up. Fred was one of the few people I knew who would stand up to Post.

I was very upset. It was OK him having a go at me, but what had my wife to do with anything? It was a snobbish remark that Post made. In Belgium and Holland street traders are looked down on, and hamburger salesmen are the worst. They make really good money, but that doesn't matter. Making money isn't as respected in Belgium and Holland as it is in America or Britain. It is more what you do that gives you social status. You could be a poor lawyer, or a rich businessman, but in your town or village the people will only call the lawyer 'Mister'.

I told Phil Anderson about what Post had said while we were driving to Milan, and he must have spoken to Post because something happened at the team meeting that night. Peter didn't exactly say he was sorry, but it came across that he was, and I ended up doing a good Milan–San Remo.

Actually, both directeurs at Panasonic were hard men in their own way. I think, in five years Walter Planckaert only said, 'Good ride' to me twice. I am trying not to be like that with my riders now. I try to give them feed-back and make them feel valued. We have a system within Davitamon where we tell everyone when they have done something correctly, as well as when they've done it wrong, even if it's something that hasn't worked. I think that is the way to be. I think it gets more results in the long run than being hard all the time.

And Post was hard. There were no excuses you could give him. No exceptions would ever be made. Well, nearly no exceptions. Post did understand when you had gone as far as you could possibly go, as I found out in the 1987 Tour de France.

To get into the Panasonic Tour team you really had to fight for selection. I did it by doing a good ride in the Tour of Switzerland in 1987, but that meant I went straight from the Tour of Switzerland to the start of the Tour, which was more than four weeks of racing with very little rest.

We had a very good team in the 1987 Tour: we had two sprinters in Vanderaerden and Planckaert; we had Phil Anderson, and we had Robert Millar for the overall. A lot of leaders, but it meant that there were very few domestiques to share the work of looking after them, so it was very hard for us. We had to ride for the sprinters; we had to ride for the team time trial; we had to ride for Anderson; and we had to ride to get Robert in a good position before the mountains.

Five days from the end I was on my knees and I still had to do a mountain stage to La Plagne, and another after that. I was absolutely wasted. It was all I could do to get to the finish, just pedal over pedal. I got to the finish, eventually, and from there somehow found my hotel room. In those days it wasn't like it is now after a stage, where the teams have a doctor and they put riders straight onto a drip to get liquids and glucose into them. All there was in those days was a bread roll on your bed.

Anyway, I ate that and crawled under the blankets. Then I cracked. I just lay under the blankets and began to cry. I had finished just inside the time limit and I couldn't get over the fact that I had to do it all again the next day. There were four mountains the next day; I didn't know how I was going to do it.

I was sharing a room with a Dutch rider, Teun Van Vliet, and he must have gone to fetch Peter, because all I was doing was sobbing under my blankets. I wouldn't come out. After a few minutes Peter came into the room and sat down on my bed. I still didn't come out, so Peter just sat there rubbing me on the back like you would comfort a child and repeating, 'It'll be all right, it'll be all right.' He did that until I felt better; so, as much as he could be a hard bastard and humiliate you in front of the other riders, he did have a soft spot, although he hid it well and you had to go through hell to find it!

The next day I was dropped on the first climb. I was the first and Urs Zimmerman, a Swiss rider who had been third in the Tour the previous year, got dropped next. He was riding about ten metres in front of me, zigzagging all over the road. Then he rode into the gutter and fell off. I went past him and Walter came up next to me in the car and said, 'Don't you think you should stop? There are four big mountains after this, and you are by yourself already.' So I stopped. I was done. They put my bike on the roof of the car and I got into the ambulance. Three days from the end of the Tour – that is a terrible feeling.

I didn't see Peter that night, and next morning Fred de Bruyne was taking me in the car to the airport in Geneva. I was just getting in the car when Peter came out of the hotel and put his arms around me. On the way to the airport, Fred took me to a restaurant on the lake and we had lunch. It was beautiful weather, and we sat outside on a sort of jetty. We had a nice meal and a really good bottle of wine, and I said, 'Fred, what are we doing here? This must be so expensive.' And Fred said, 'No, it's OK. Peter said I had to take you out for lunch.' Peter understood that I couldn't have finished the Tour; I couldn't have climbed those mountains and finished in the time limit. He understood that I had given everything for the team.

Essentially, that 1987 Tour de France experience is an illustration of what being a good domestique in cycling is all about. You have to put the team before your personal ambitions. On the one hand, there is personal glory of finishing the Tour, no matter what position you are in. On the other, the feeling of stopping with three days to go is totally bleak, totally without any personal glory. In fact, after I arrived home in 1987 I was so ashamed that I hid in my house, not wanting to see or talk to anyone. It is such a temptation to save something so that you make it to Paris, but that isn't why you are being paid. You must give everything, and if that means you can't finish, then so be it.

If I look back at Post, and I look at the job I have now, and at our management team at Davitamon-Lotto, maybe if we lack one thing it is the ability to wield the iron rod. But having said that, I'm not sure that this generation of riders would respond to it. Times have changed and maybe Post wouldn't have been a good directeur today, or he would have had to change the way he was.

The kids today seem to need more support; they need you to be there for them, and they respond positively to support. You can tell from their voices that they react to someone taking an interest. When people take an interest in what you are doing it is very gratifying. When I was racing there weren't any mobile 'phones, but even then you hardly got a call from a directeur, or anybody connected with the team, asking how it was going. Post's theory was if you are a pro, you do your job. And if you don't do your job, you go.

But from what I've seen over the years, if you want to get the best out of your riders, which is what your aim should be because your sponsors are investing money in them, then it is up to you to at least find a way of extracting that money's worth from your riders. Now the way I do that might not be Post's way, or Walter Godefroot's way, because within a general framework for being a good directeur you have to put your own stamp on how you do things.

Having said that, I learned a lot from Peter Post. One thing with him was that nothing was too good for us. One year we changed tracksuit suppliers five times, because the tracksuits either didn't fit or they weren't made out of good material. He was like that with everything. We had the best of everything, and you really appreciate that.

Little things take on really big proportions in a pro bike rider's life. Just before the 1987 Tour I had a frame made in Australia out of 753 special light tubing, and I took it to Eddy Merckx, who was our bike supplier and asked him to paint it in the team colours. But Eddy said he wouldn't do it because his company hadn't made it. I was really disappointed. I told him I'd had the frame made in special light tubing just for the Tour. But Eddy said, 'That's OK, I'll make you one.' And he did, and I started the Tour de France on a special light bike made by Eddy Merckx out of 753 tubing. Now, for a domestique in those days that was a big lift.

I encountered a new sort of freedom with Post as well. With Peugeot there was always a big brother attitude, someone looking over your shoulder, checking and criticising. Post treated us all like grown-ups. We were professionals, so he trusted us to live and train like professionals. If you weren't on the team racing, he didn't give you training schedules to complete, or anything like that. If you weren't getting results, or not working well in support of the leaders, he would just kick you out of the team at the end of the year.

In my first year on the team I rode the Giro d'Italia and did a lot of work for Vanderaerden, but I didn't get a ride in the Tour de France. I was OK with that as I'd already experienced the Tour with Peugeot, and there is a lot of suffering for a rider like me to get over the mountains.

I rode two kermesse races in the week after the Giro, then I had six weeks before I was needed again by Panasonic for a race. I had a two week rest, then began training again, put in some long rides and rode one race a week. But in all that time I didn't have one 'phone call from Post or anyone else from Panasonic. I think his idea that you are a professional and it's up to you to come up with the goods is OK, but you do need some support from time to time. Maybe just a phone call or a friendly message. I am trying to do that now. I don't want to be on top of my riders, but I sense they need support and I try to be there for them.

The freedom Peter gave me did me one big favour in 1987: it allowed me to ride the first Kellogg's Tour of Britain. It was incredible. I rode for the Ever Ready team, wearing their top and a pair of Panasonic shorts. I don't think that would be allowed now. I won the first stage into Newcastle in the north east of England, and that was a real thrill. The next stage was a quite hilly one, going across the Pennines to Manchester. The organisers had put a team together for me, just for the Kellogg's Tour, with Ferdi Van den Haute and another Belgian called Dick Wijnenberg. It wasn't a strong team for the hills, and my old Peugeot team, which I think was Z-Peugeot by then, attacked on every climb with the idea of getting rid of me. In the end they managed it, and Malcolm Elliott went away with Joey Mcloughlin and another rider, and gained five minutes.

I was devastated by that. Sean Kelly was there in the bunch with his Kas team, and I was riding on the front on my own trying to bring the break back, but no-one came up and offered to give me a hand.

That night I saw Kelly eating with his team and I said, 'Why didn't you ride. You just let the race go like that. It was the second stage, you were still in contention and yet you let them ride away.' And all Kelly said was, 'Why didn't you ask?' That stopped me. Why didn't I ask? I never even thought of asking. It was another wake up.

Kelly was such a professional, a complete rider with one foot in the old school and one in the new. Look at the races he won. I don't think that there has been such a complete rider in cycling since him. You couldn't help but have respect for him, and he was such a hard bastard as well. Physically strong, but hard. He also had a calm savvy about him that earned respect. He had the aura that makes a difference with a champion, makes them even more respected by the other riders. Miguel Induráin had that as well.

Kelly used to let a race happen, let it unfold. I could never do that. I would always try to make a race go my way, but when you do that you don't flow any more. Frans Maassen once said to me, 'You know the trouble with you, Allan? You are too nervous. You should relax more in the races.' Kelly didn't actually relax, but he allowed the race to unfold, flowed with it and re-adjusted his insights or his tactics to adapt to the changes. I couldn't do that.

When you hear him commentating on the television today, his insights on the tactics, on what is happening, his analysis of situations is spot-on. Kelly was always a good leader, too. He let races unfold, but he was always up front, where his domestiques could see him, which makes them more committed to do their bit. It's a bit like warriors fighting harder when they can see their flag up with them at the battle front.

Actually, I had very little to do with Kelly when I was racing. There is a strong class system in the peloton, with the top riders forming an upper class. Then there are the middle class and lower classes, and you tend to only interact with your own class. I remember being upset once in the Tour of Flanders when I was in the front group and Adri Van der Poel said to Kelly; 'Look at all these second-row riders who are at the front. Look at Peiper – he'll be dropped on the next climb.'

I took offence at that and I ended up in the front group of ten in the finale, looking after Vanderaerden. Criquielion had a flat at the top of the Muur and changed wheels. In those days we only had seven speed blocks, so if you had the 12 you didn't have the 23. When 'Criq' changed wheels they put in a 12, meaning that when he attacked at the top of the Bosberg he had a 12, which gave him a higher gear, and I was chasing with a 13. From the Bosberg to the finish it is mostly downhill.

Criquielion won, but he got done a favour: the chase from behind wasn't as committed as it could have been. It is the same with every generation – a top guy will do a favour one day for another top man, and they expect it to be re-paid. 'Criq's' past favours were repaid that day. That never happened with Panasonic, though. We were the best, and got no favours. Teams often worked together to make sure we didn't win. Imagine going into a race with that attitude.

The biggest rivalry in cycling while I was racing was between Post and Jan Raas. Raas' teams definitely went into every race with the intention of making Panasonic lose. In fact, that rivalry eventually caused my demise at Panasonic and changed my whole career.

16

Davitamon-Lotto

It's been six months since I started my job as team director with Davitamon-Lotto. It was a new start for me, a dream job, but I didn't have any false pretences about how I got it. I got lucky. Lucky in the sense that I was in the right place at the right time. I'm not saying that I don't think I have the qualities to do it, because I know I have. The job is in me. I just had the cards on my side, and of that I am only too well aware, but at the same time I am grateful for the opportunity.

In the twelve years since I stopped racing I have been on a search for myself, a search to find peace with my past and to find out who I am. The search has taken me to India twice, to America twice and seen years of early morning meditation between 4 am and 6 am. I had a dedication to my practice which paralleled the dedication I had during my cycling career. I read lots of books and went on numerous courses to help me understand myself and the ghosts I carried around with me, the ones that had cast their shadow over my true self and affected my every day life.

Probably the most important thing I learnt was the ability to be aware of my own thoughts, feelings and spoken words. It wasn't an easy thing to learn, I can tell you that. Standing back and analysing what you say, what you think and how you react was of monumental importance to me, because once you have learnt to be aware of those things, then you can be responsible for them. Not that taking responsibility is easy. You become keenly aware of your weaknesses as a human being, and you see more of the side-shows going on in other people's lives.

One evening recently at a race in France I was having an after-dinner drink with some of the personnel, and during the conversation one of the masseurs said to me that I only saw the good side of people. He said that I should be careful I didn't get myself into trouble with that.

Now if he had said the opposite, that would have worried me. Later in the evening I saw him again. This time we were alone, so I asked him what he would like me to say about him if ever I was talking with some others and he wasn't there. If they were talking about his defects, would he rather me talk about his qualities, or just join in with the general negativity? I told him I knew his negative points, and he knew mine. As long as we could work together in peace while acknowledging those weaker traits, why would we need to emphasize them? Instead, emphasising qualities creates positive energy, and positive energy builds and creates, whereas negative energy divides and separates. People's egos, you know the bit of us that doesn't always need our permission to do things, love to divide and separate through judgement and negativity, and in a team of 53 that can undermine team spirit in such an insidious way that nobody even senses the downward spiral.

It hasn't been easy to find my place in the team. Firstly I had to learn everything from new. Then I saw that there was a framework in which I had to work, but once I had that down I realized that every director puts his own stamp on the job. I needed to do that.

My philosophy with the team is that positive creates unity, and negative creates division. Our team is a pyramid, with our manager, Marc Sergeant, at the top and the four of us directors unified under him, and then that unity filters down through the personnel to the riders. The riders win the races, of course, but the unity of the directors creates the right environment for them to win.

The one thing I saw from my days with Panasonic was that Walter Planckaert was faithful to Peter Post to the letter. So much so that behind his back the riders used to call him Walter Post. When I signed my contract for this year, my priority was to Marc Sergeant, I wanted to be as faithful to him as Walter was to Peter. I had felt the strength of their unity, but I also felt they had missed a twist – they didn't always display an empathy with their riders. We needed someone to do that.

The four of us team directors answer to Marc, but he gives us total freedom and stands behind our decisions. I could see that we all had the qualities to do our jobs, but we also had different strengths, and I put the point across time after time at meetings that we had to support each other's weaker points. It's the same in a marriage: if you can put ego aside, support weaknesses and appreciate strengths, then together you are stronger than both of you individually.

Hendrick Redant is super-intellectual, fantastic at logistics and tactics, but he will admit himself that he lacks the ability to feel. That's the thing I am good at. I see the riders faces in a morning, feel their energy and gauge their mental state. I can also sense friction and build bridges in a subtle way. Hendrick and I work great as a team. He has supported me, helped me learn and I affirm his qualities, because even the boss needs praise from time to time.

Davitamon-Lotto has brought sense to my life, a place to use the answers to some of the questions I've been asking myself for years. Everything I've been through helps me in my job, and the role I've found within the management team. Asking myself all those questions has given me the insight to see, feel and hear what is happening around me. To be the bridge between two land masses, to unite so that we can conquer is the role I've found. Every day I get out the iron and flatten the creases in the fabric of the team.

17

Dr Janssen

I won a few races at the end of 1986: I won the G P Impanis, a stage in the Tour of Belgium and a few others. It was like my career was moving on to another level. I'd had my time in Peugeot concentrating on prologues and time trials, moved on to being a good domestique in the best team, and I had begun to focus on the Classics. Maybe I could be a contender.

I stayed in Belgium during the winter, training hard with Marc Sergeant, who was then the Champion of Belgium. It was a very cold winter. One day I remember it was minus 17 degrees and Marc had a puncture not far from where he lived. He got off and said, 'Oh I'm not changing this,' and he just rode home on the flat. There was a lot of ice and I crashed a lot.

We didn't have home-trainers with resistance; we only had rollers, and they were useless for getting any strength. You had to go out on the road, so I just used to wrap up in a lot of clothes. Actually, I didn't mind riding in minus temperatures. It's worse when it's two degrees and raining. At least that winter it was dry.

The training paid off and I was beginning to go well, when one day I was riding over towards Aalst and the flap of one of those tents that telephone engineers put up over where they're working blew up in the wind and into my front wheel. I went straight over the handlebars and landed on my back. I got up, but it was all I could do to crawl home on my bike; my back was killing me.

I had to go to a training camp in Spain the next day, but when I got there I couldn't ride my bike at all and they wouldn't let me come home. That was the old mentality – they just kept me there hoping it would get better. There was never any thought about getting something sorted out in the old days. It was always trust to luck; it'll get better on its own. But very often things don't get better on their own. That is another attitude that has changed today, thankfully.

Anyway, I stayed for a week down at the training camp, just convalescing basically, when I should have been at the physio. After that I came back to Belgium and started going to the physio. My first race was Het Volk, and the other guys had ten or 15 races in their legs already, but because I'd started later and missed out a couple of weeks training, I seemed to have more in reserve.

Phil Anderson had a trainer here in Belgium, and he was working with him using new ways – interval training and a heart rate monitor. Things they do all the time today, but it was only in baby shoes back then. We both did a lactate test, but when I started training like Phil my results hadn't come back yet, so I had to train using his values. That meant that I was doing intervals at Phil's threshold, which was my maximum heart rate!

Still, it made a hell of a difference, training like that, but we really went at it. Hard days back to back, riding behind a derny at 55 kph. Like I said this type of training was only in its baby shoes, an experiment, and the guy we were working with hadn't factored in any recovery time yet.

To give you an idea of what we trained like, after Milan–San Remo I had a day off on the Sunday. Then we went out for five hours on the Monday, did two interval sessions on the Tuesday and Wednesday, then rode the Dwars door Vlaanderen on the Thursday, where the purpose was just to finish. We had an easy day on Friday, rode the Grand Prix E3–Harelbeke on the Saturday, had an easy day behind the derny on Sunday. Easy on Monday, then ride the Three Days of De Panne. After that it was two easy days, then the Tour of Flanders.

It was really, really intensive. I remember doing one session where I rode out for an hour, did a five minute climb at a very high intensity, rode 14 minutes in the big ring around a lap to get to the bottom of the same climb, and go up it again. I repeated that five or six times, before riding back home, and that would be a four-hour ride. One night, after I'd done a session like that, I got up out of bed to go to the toilet, walked out of the room in the dark and smashed my head on the door jamb. I couldn't wake up, and I went into the toilet and pissed next to the toilet on the floor.

I was so tired, but if you train like that and you rest up a little bit, you get super-compensation. And with me, it worked: it took me to the next level and made the difference in a Classic from just missing the break to being with it. I finished 10th in the 1987 Tour of Flanders – my best ride in a Classic at that stage of my career.

The training changed my career dramatically. I was nearly there and started thinking of doing even better. But after the Classics in 1987 my form suddenly went right down. I had no energy at all, and the reason was that to train like I had been doing, you are using more than you've got. I had flattened my batteries and needed time to re-charge them. A couple of years later Peter Post said to me, 'You know, if you keep training like you are training, you won't be racing much longer.' Actually, I was quite proud he said that, because most directeurs criticise their riders for not training hard enough.

Doing those rides, being in the break in Milan–San Remo and Tour of Flanders in 1987, and doing well in the next few years in those races and in De Panne, Paris–Roubaix and Ghent–Wevelgem, meant that I'd sort of found a place within the season that was mine. So from then on, that was when I had to be good and it was what I focused everything on – my bike training, my gym training, everything.

My career had evolved. I had done my apprenticeship in the first years with Peugeot, found out the framework of my job, become meticulous in everything I did. I had found my place as a domestique with Panasonic, and now I had found my space in the season as a rider. It had taken me five years, half a career, but that is how long it takes. Even now you see pros winning, who have ten years experience or more, and maybe don't have such strong legs any more, simply because of all the savvy they have built up.

But even with Panasonic I was still learning. I learned an incredible amount from the soigneurs in that team. We didn't have doctors in cycling teams when I was racing, well not on a day to day basis travelling with the team, like they do now. But I think that the soigneurs at Panasonic were nearly as good as doctors, and in some respects better. They seemed to understand better how various vitamins, treatments and medicines interacted with each other and affected your body. Maybe it was because they massaged your legs every day, they could feel when things had changed, and could feel the effects of anything they'd given you. Also, I think it was because they saw the rider all through the year: they saw you when you were good, when you were down, and when you were tired.

It meant that when doctors did come on the scene in the late eighties and early nineties, there wasn't much faith in them. I remember one doctor coming to a training camp in the South of France, and he'd brought a suitcase full of cortisone with him. We thought he was bringing vitamins and things to support us through the season, and all he'd brought was cortisone, just a drug. Now that's not caring for your health, so no wonder no one had faith in him.

With the soigneur who looked after me at Panasonic, I had a gentlemen's agreement that he wouldn't do anything to enhance my performance without discussing it with me first. I don't know whether he kept his side of it – to be honest, I never asked. His job was to keep my body performing to its maximum potential, and the problem with that is pressure from above.

I remember one team in Tirreno–Adriatico, where the soigneurs woke all the riders up at one o'clock in the morning and gave them an iron injection, just because the manager had been getting it in the neck from the sponsors, and he was getting nervous.

It was insanity to have that kind of power over someone's health, but that was the era, that was what it was like. What a contrast to today, when I look at the way the doctors in our team work with the riders. There is absolute trust; the riders trust them not only with their health but with family problems, with their weaknesses and with their fears. The doctors are there first and foremost for the riders now, not for the team.

There is a whole lot more care about the riders now, and I really think we are through the worst of the drugs era. The UCI have these health books, and do out-of-race controls, as well as controls at the races. It's not perfect, and I have concerns that you will read about later, but it is holding everyone a bit more in line. Whereas in my day it was basically a free-for-all.

And rules are the only way to do it: people will cheat otherwise. I know a kid who doesn't live far from me, and when they brought out that book by Willy Voet, which documented all the ways he had helped bike riders to cheat the dope controls over the years, this kid went out and bought it and copied everything in the book. Sometimes cyclists get criticised when we react badly to insiders telling tales about what has gone on behind closed doors. It's called spitting in the soup. But with that kid I know, and many others like him you can bet, how responsible was Voet to write his book? There are two sides to everything is all I'm saying.

You will not clean the sport up completely. I am fairly certain doping isn't institutionalised in the big teams any more, like it was with Festina. The cost of a positive result would be ruinous for a ProTour team like ours, but individuals will try. Everyone is looking for a boost, and I was the same. Once I visited an osteopath and he suggested I try taking arnica, because it was good for the heart and my circulation. So on a long training ride I tried it, taking a few drops from a little bottle of arnica every 30 minutes. I could feel a definite kick and started using it before prologues.

But instead of taking ten drops, I was just taking swigs out of the bottle during the 30 minutes before a prologue. It definitely helped, and this is the problem. Arnica wasn't on any banned list, but it helped and I was over-dosing on it, and that is why the authorities have to keep up their vigilance on the sport. They mustn't rest, because it is human nature that if you find an advantage you're not going to tell anyone about it – you're going to use it, and use it a lot. Now, if that product is also dangerous, you have a problem.

There were some doctors in the past who really cared and who the riders trusted, even when I was racing. At Panasonic we worked with a Dutch doctor, Dr Janssen, and it was his theory that there had to be some common ground between what was doping and what was therapeutic care of the riders. For example, there came a time when any artificial administration of testosterone was banned, but it's a medical fact that when testosterone levels fall the body is damaged by racing. He thought that keeping the body levels of some substances within a safe band was beneficial to a rider's health, given that his profession demands that he can't just go home because he's tired.

Dr Janssen viewed everything from a health perspective, rather than just giving you stuff to boost your performance. For instance, when he first examined me, my vitamin B12 levels were sky high, so he stopped me getting any extra B12 until they came down. And as my levels came down I began to go better. My legs got more supple, I got faster and faster, and it culminated with a stage win in the Tour of Italy.

I was within the levels and I won a stage in the Tour of Italy, so what Dr Janssen was doing makes logical sense to me. He stopped giving me something, and I went better. I remember riders talking about EPO and saying that when you used it, you got out of bed and you weren't smashed any more, and provided you kept within the haematocrit levels the UCI set, EPO was a good thing. But there is so much discrepancy about what levels are safe, what can be used and what can't be used, which is one reason I think it's not good to say a safe haematocrit level for everyone is 50. For example, where someone might have a natural level of 44, a level where his body works in harmony, if he then manipulates that figure upwards that could be dangerous for him, even though he may still be below 50.

I think that was what Dr Janssen was trying to get across, and why these UCI health books are so good, is because they get a profile of a rider's normal levels and so they can investigate any fluctuations – and they do. Believe me, if anyone shows fluctuations now they go under the microscope. But the whole question of doping and health is one that nobody has all the answers to, least of all me. In fact, cyclists are probably the last people to ask, because we get so obsessed about our careers and our bodies that the whole world, and our place in it, tends to fall out of focus.

Often you couldn't even have a conversation with anyone in the bunch if it wasn't about bikes. Everything was about cycling, or more often about their cycling and their place within the sport. That is how self-obsessed you have to be, but I can remember thinking, 'I'll be glad when I retire so I can have a conversation with some of these guys'.

I was riding the Tour of Italy one year, and Jean-Marie Wampers was complaining about his shorts. They were either too long, or too short, or too tight, but whatever. All he could talk about every day was his shorts. Then came the day after an earth quake in Albania, and Jean-Marie was still banging on about his shorts. Peter Winnen, a Dutch rider who was in the Panasonic team said to him, 'Christ, 35,000 people got killed yesterday and all you can do is moan about your shorts.' It wasn't meant personally, but that really brought something home to me. It was probably the first time I stopped and thought that there are other things in the world than me whinging about riding my bike. Peter thought about those sorts of things a lot.

Looking back, 1987 and 1988 were the best two years of my racing career, but I was expecting more. I was really hard on myself, wanting more all the time. I was hard on those around me, too. I think I am a lot better now, I hope so anyway. I think that the events of the last few years have changed me.

But I was incredibly driven in those days, and can remember yelling at riders during races. Peter Post once said that you need to be out of cycling for a while before you become a directeur sportif, and he's right. Towards the end of my racing career I got a call from Jim Ochowiz asking me if I wanted to be a directeur at Motorola. I wanted to race for one more year, so I said no. Maybe I made a mistake, who knows? I have come back into the sport now as a directeur with so much enthusiasm, whereas when I finished racing I was just burned. There was hardly any enthusiasm left at all. I had all my own frustrations, too. I hadn't learnt to deal with my own life yet, so how could I help someone deal with theirs?

If I had stayed in cycling I would have missed a lot of the experiences that have made me who I am today. Working for myself in another business, exploring my spirituality, shaving all my hair off, meditating and going to India, all things that have helped me find out who I am. And they will help me do the work I'm doing now.

Somebody asked me the other day, with all the things I'd done in my life, how could I go back into the restricted, sometimes crooked, world of professional cycling? But maybe coming from outside almost, I can do some good. Maybe I can find a new, productive and stimulating way of doing things.

18

Tyler and Danilo

There are times in life when your courage and inner strength are tested to the limit. Times when life's circumstances are out of your control, and all you can do is ride the wave until you hit the shore. Often you know you are right, but cannot exonerate yourself. And sometimes life is just a jumble of all these things. It was like that when I was racing, and it's like that now in my new job as a team director. You have a lot of responsibility, but sometimes you feel in freefall, floating about on other people's wants and whims.

Every morning when I'm away with the team I get up at around 6 am and go for a run. It is the only time of the day I can call my own, and the hour I give myself to enjoy a purely physical activity is holy. It keeps me grounded and sane. To get my clothes on, running shoes and my earphones with my favourite tunes, and hammer myself for 30 to 60 minutes is what balances out the rest of my day. It is my time, while the rest of the day I belong to everybody else.

As early as 7 am I need to be on call because of the possibility of one of our riders being required for a random dope test. The inspectors call by cell phone, or knock on the director's door to tell you which rider or riders they want, and you then have 15 minutes to get them downstairs for a blood test. Outside that time, and it is treated as a positive test.

The noose is being drawn tighter, and the riders who will benefit from this new stringency will be the young ones. For some of the older riders, it will be more difficult to produce the results they did without the chemical enhancement of the products they used in the 1990s. Random tests at races, out-of-competition control for those riders who are on a strictly controlled list, like medal winners, top ten ranked riders, or those on a black list because of irregular blood values in the past. Plus testing after races, and the use of compulsory health books, where everything a rider uses must be entered. All these things are cleaning up the sport.

Yet there are some things that worry me. The Tyler Hamilton affair of 2004, and the Danillo Hondo positive in the Tour of Murcia 2005, for me both leave questions about this new era of stringent control and zero-tolerance punishment. Hondo's national federation has, for some reason, lessened his sentence from two years to one, against the wishes of the UCI. Why is that? On the face of it, Hondo can resume his career after one year, but the ProTour charter states that he cannot join a ProTour team, so his career could be severely jeopardised. And Hamilton? I just don't feel that the case against him is proved beyond all doubt, but he still has been punished as if it were.

During the Giro d'Italia this year two of the Spanish Liberty Seguros team went over the 50 mark for haematocrit level. Both were suspended by their team, after receiving from the UCI a mandatory period when they weren't allowed to compete because of being 'unhealthy'. One of those riders was subsequently fired by his team, and had his name dragged through the press as a drugs user. Then his B sample tested negative (each person giving a haematocrit above 50 is blood-tested for drugs, and the blood taken split into A and B samples – both samples must be positive for the sample to be accepted as positive). Now he has no team, and not much left of his name.

The Hondo case has intrigued me from the start. He is a great sprinter, and showed that with his second place in Milan–San Remo this year. He earned a lot of money as a racer, and had lucrative modelling contracts. So why would he use an outdated Russian amphetamine which, although it is still on the banned list, is not available in any western European product? Either he was ill-informed, stupid, or both. Or even innocent perhaps?

Amphetamines are gone, a thing of the past. Plus the dose he tested positive for in Murcia was minute, and he only provided one positive test, but he was tested several times during that race. Why, in these times of highly publicised rigour, use a tiny amount of a stone-age drug on one day of a stage race that you were doing well in and so were bound to be tested?

People go to Death Row all the time for murders they didn't commit, but although cycling punishments aren't a death sentence, a person's livelihood, and all they ever stood for as a human being, could be washed away in an instant. The new controls are fantastic, but there is no room for discussion any more.

Zero-tolerance is good in theory, but it makes victims as well. Perhaps the worst thing about Hondo's positive was that it didn't even make the headlines. The career of a great, previously clean, rider was gone, and nobody cared. Maybe there is an inside story I am not privy to, but if there isn't we are on the wrong track. There are always other explanations for a positive like his – something in the food chain, or sabotage, for instance. Sounds crazy? Yes, but you could liquidate a whole team if you were serious. The riders test positive, the team loses its licence and the ProTour is one team less. It's a real danger, and yet there is still no room for discussion.

For a rider, testing positive is a devastating thing to happen and, set against the background of sport's drug-ridden history, it is devastating even if you are guilty. After all, you have only done something that many others before you have done, and got away with. But to test positive and be innocent, to have your life's work taken away, is something from which you would never recover. Then there is the question of what is on the banned list, and what isn't. When I raced in the 80s and 90s two great riders tested positive for substances that were later taken off the list.

Eddy Planckaert was positive for an anti-influenza tablet he had taken before what is now known as the Dwars door Vlaanderen – a Belgium semi-classic which is ten days before the Tour of Flanders. It was bad weather and Eddy was wary of getting sick and ruining his form for Flanders and Roubaix, his main goals for the season. His name was spread all over the newspapers and on television, but two years later the substance he tested positive for was dropped from the banned list. And it probably never helped him anyway. Even more ludicrous was the positive test of double World Champion and Tour of Italy winner, Gianni Bugno, for being over the limit for caffeine – a substance later removed from the list, although there have been calls recently to re-instate it.

For those two riders today, a positive test would mean the end of their careers. Who is to say that products now on the list won't be taken off the list in future? Maybe even the drug that ended Hondo's career will be taken off. I am not saying I am against drug testing and regulations. Far from it. I just want to say that every case isn't the same, there are grey areas. Zero-tolerance sends a strong message, but it can be wrong, and it isn't the only way in every case.

Back in the early 80s when I turned pro, there was a saying in the bunch that if you had never been positive you were never any good. Like I have said before, doping and amphetamines were a joke, no more serious than truancy or drinking from your dad's whiskey bottle. On top of that, doctors were the friends of some riders, and some looked the other way during the dope controls. All in the name of the sport we love.

In 1986 I was not selected for the Panasonic team for the Tour de France. We had a 'gun team' that year, with a lot of top riders, and there was no place for me. I was still finding my feet with Panasonic, finding my role and my place, as well as still learning how I could reap the best results with the ability I had.

I rode the Tour of Italy that year, raced for another two weeks then because I had no National Championships to go for, unlike the rest of Europe, I then rested for two weeks after that. I trained really hard while the Tour de France was on, doing two or three seven-hour rides during the week and racing a Kermesse every Sunday, just to hammer myself. On that regime I took fourth in the Tour of Denmark, and my form was rising in time for the objective I'd picked for myself – the Tour of Belgium. I had learned enough to know by now that I couldn't win against the best riders when they were peaking, so the next best thing was to get them while they were down, and after the Tour de France is a good time to do that.

The Tour of Belgium started with a prologue, and I was good at those. The night before we heard from our director, Walter Planckaert, that there was going to be a doping control after every stage, but I lost the prologue by a fraction of a second, and there was no control. Typical of the era, I thought. And I was doubly furious because the rider who beat me was an old dog, and to rub salt into my wounds he told me years later that he had paid the warning motorcyclist in front of him to slow down on each corner so he could slipstream out of it.

I saw the devastation on the face of Australian Michael Rodgers, and felt his helplessness when he lost the Tour of Switzerland on the last climb this year, and I remembered how I felt after the Tour of Belgium prologue, and when I was flicked from victory in the Franco-Belge. I know losing is part of sport, but when you have a win taken from you it's hard to gut, and when it's done unfairly it makes it worse. The unspoken pro ethic of no-blame because we all have free choice is sorely tested at times.

So the promise of doping controls after each stage of the Tour of Belgium was a joke after the prologue. The next three stages passed without us ever seeing a control doctor on the race. Then on stage four I got away in a small group as we crossed the Ardennes. Nico Verhoeven won the stage, and I was second. After the stage we all grouped around Walter to see if any of us had to go to the control, but he said not, so we rode the five kilometres to our hotel at Han-Sur-Lesse.

At about ten that evening, Walter came into my room and asked if I had been to the doping control, and I told him no and that he had said none of us had to go. He was new at being a director, and was working alone, like they used to. On top of that, he had no mobile phone or GPS to help him out, like we have today. I can understand that he was trying to slide the blame onto me, but whoever was to blame we still had a problem.

Dirk Nachtergaele, who has been the masseur of Planckaert, Vanderaerden, Museeuw and now Boonen, was my masseur then, and he had massive experience in running a team. He advised Walter to ring the doctor who had done the control, which he did and, against all the procedures, we were allowed to go to his house, 60 kilometres away in Namur, next morning to give my sample. That was how the doctors were in those days – sometimes in your favour and sometimes against, but always human.

I got up at 5 am to give my sample in Namur, and after that we had a double-stage. The first one was a mini Liège–Bastogne–Liège, and then we had a time trial in the afternoon that was likely to decide the race, because the final day was relatively easy. It was murder: time after time I got dropped on the hills as the Lotto team, lead by Belgian National Champion, Marc Sergeant, tried to unload me. They knew I would be a danger in the afternoon time trial, and could take the overall classification.

My team-mate, a young Dutchman called Gert-Jan Theunisse, who would later go on to greatness in the Tour de France and get caught up in numerous doping scandals himself, was looking after me and keeping me in his wheel as he made the tempo for me on each climb so I wouldn't end up too far behind at the top. Then on the descents we would get back to the front group, only to repeat the process on the next climb.

After one such climb, we made contact with the front at the bottom of the descent and I came out from behind Gert-Jan and hit them from behind with all I'd got. Nobody could react, and I got away. The Lotto team chased for 40 kilometres and blew themselves apart, but they couldn't catch me and I won on my own at the top of the climb in St Hubert by 20 seconds from Sergeant.

On the podium I received the flowers for winning, but couldn't understand why they weren't giving me the leader's jersey. There had been a discussion and Sergeant's director, Walter Goodefroot, who is now with T-Mobile, had made a complaint about my late dope test. As a result I was handed a ten-minute time penalty, which was out of context with what the rule book said should happen.

I was devastated. The Tour of Belgium was my home race – well, as near to a home race in Europe. That afternoon I had no motivation and finished the time trial in fourth place. The decision was out of my hands and none of my doing; the Belgians had pulled together to wipe out the Aussie in a Dutch team.

Earlier this year I told my associate director at Davitamon-Lotto, Hendrick Redant, that when I raced I had to do twice as much as the other riders in a team to get recognition, because I was a foreigner. He laughed then, but last week when we met for a coffee before he went off to the Tour de France he said that he had understood what I meant, but now I had to do three times as much because I couldn't talk with my legs any more.

Three weeks ago we were at the Dauphiné Libéré, where we won a stage with Axel Merckx, in typical gutsy Merckx style, and we had Wim Van Huffel attack 12 kilometres from the top of the Ventoux and only get caught by Vinokourov in the last 1,500 metres. The team was making an impression.

In a conversation at the Dauphiné, with the head of marketing of one of our sponsors and another of our co-directors, Herman Frison, we were discussing the question of taking a Belgian or an Australian helper on the Tour de France. The marketing man's opinion was, 'Why would we want to take a foreigner when we can take a Belgian?' I was nailed to the floor. That's how precarious my position is now, and how it was back when I raced.

The day after the 1986 Tour of Belgium was a Monday, and there had been no written news for two days. Then came the headlines; 'PEIPER POSITIVE – Verhoven wins'. I had lost the Tour of Belgium, and now I was being stripped of my dignity and had my name turned to shit. It went around the world too, and even made the headlines in Melbourne, my home-town, where cycling only used to get a by-line.

My Flemish mother-in-law wrote to the journalist who made the headline, Harry van den Bremdt – I never forgot his name. She even telephoned the paper. I was positive without even knowing the test result. I started the Tour of Holland the next week, but I was a shell. It was a devastating time for me.

Five months later the Belgian Cycling Federation made a deal with Peter Post, my director at Panasonic. My sample had been negative, and even though the doctor had done the test outside the time limit it was still considered valid. I should have got my ten minutes back, but the Belgian Federation said they would only declare me negative if I didn't appeal to gain my time back.

Two weeks later a rectification of my positive test was submitted in the Belgian Federation magazine. Inside the back cover, in two short, small print lines I was vindicated, released from Death Row.

You can't make it right, you can't defend yourself, and nobody will stand up for you. Is it because I am a foreigner? You know as a 17 year old I used to have the name 'Foreign Lice' thrown at me by parents, supporters and riders alike here in Belgium. It seemed that there was no one who would make a stand for me. Sometimes I'm not sure that there is now.

19

Neil Stephens

Back in 1986 I went home to Australia to ride the Herald Sun Tour. I've explained in earlier chapters about my relationship with Australian cycling, about how I hadn't been selected for Australian teams. So for me to go back to Australia and race, it was like a chance to go back to my home-town and show them what I could do.

I rode for an Australian sponsor in a team specially put together for the race, with two Australian pros, Neil Stephens and my friend Gary Trowell, and a couple of other riders.

We started well, I won the prologue and had the leader's jersey for four or five days. Neil Stephens won the time trial stage, and then came the mountain stages. On the day before the first one I was still in the jersey, and we had Gary Trowell away in a break with a Dutch rider. Gary didn't do any work because he was protecting my overall lead, but they still won by a couple of minutes and he took over the leader's jersey.

Next day we had some really big climbs. We had to ride 40 kilometres to the base of the first mountain and then we started climbing. It was already snowing at the base, so we were climbing up this mountain with snow falling, and Neil Stephens started attacking. He attacked five or six times, until there was only three of us left with him; me, Malcolm Elliott, and Gary Trowell.

Neil attacked again, and Malcolm and I accelerated, but in doing so we dropped Gary. We were holding Neil at about 200 metres when the stage got cancelled about half way up the mountain because there was too much snow. But because he had dropped Gary at the time the race was stopped, Neil took over the jersey.

We had a big argument after that. I said to Neil: 'Look, you've been riding quietly for five days just waiting for the opportunity to attack on this big mountain. You haven't let us see your cards before, you haven't said anything to us. Gary had the leader's jersey; you should have been working for him. You haven't been truthful about your intentions.' It got very heated and we nearly came to blows, Neil and I.

Next day we had a stage down to a place called Morwell, and I told Gary: 'Coming into the finale you've just got to attack as many times as you can.' So he attacked ten or 20 times going over these rolling hills in the run-in to the finish, and everyone was chasing him down.

The thing is, Neil Stephens was still living in Australia, and I wasn't accepted as an Australian any more, I had been away for too long a time. That is what they think in Australia: if you live overseas you are not really one of us. Gary was my friend so I suppose they regarded him as a 'foreigner' by association.

Neil had the Australian riders in his pocket, plus he'd managed to pull in the European riders as well. So after Gary's final attack, I attacked and got 20 seconds, and the whole field chased.

They caught me going into the final circuits, but afterwards we had a team meeting in the back of the camper van that we were using as a mobile base, and Neil said to me and Gary: 'If you don't stop attacking me I'm not going to share my prize money with you.' I said: 'I don't care about prize money, I've won more prize money than you anyway.' A few more words went to and fro, but we made a truce that we wouldn't attack each other any more and Neil won overall with me second and Gary fourth.

Neil and I didn't get on after that, and again we didn't clear the air. He didn't talk about it, and neither did I. It was the same as with Rudy Dhaenens, we turned away from each other. But it left a very bitter feeling with me.

The funny thing is, two years later, when the World Championships were held in Ronse, Stevo and I patched things over. Before that we had ridden the Tour of Italy together, and although we didn't talk about what had happened in Australia, we did clear the air. So I asked Neil to come to Belgium to ride the World Championships for me later in the year, which he did. I offered him $6,000 to work for me in the race.

I didn't ride the Tour de France in 1988, but I was going very well after it finished. I was third in the Tour of Belgium and fourth in the Tour of Denmark. Going into the World Championships I was one of the favourites. Not one of the big favourites, but a rider who would be expected to figure.

Then shortly before the Worlds Peter Post rang me up and said he'd give me 100,000 Gilders if I won the title, which was a lot of money in 1988. But I know Post: he hadn't offered me that money because he thought I could win. He offered it to me because he didn't want Phil Anderson to win, and he knew I was going well enough to help him. Phil had left Panasonic and gone to TVM, their Dutch rivals. The offer of money was just to divide the Australian camp. Phil was going well; he lived, like I did, about 20 kilometres from Ronse, but Post didn't want another Dutch team to have the World Champion.

I'd already read between the lines, and when we got to the changing rooms in Ronse on the morning of the race, the Australian team had a meeting. Neil had already been with me for a couple of days; we'd been out training together and he'd been to my masseur. We'd talked about exactly what we were going to do in the race, but in the changing rooms the other Australians were sat around, and one of them said: 'What's going to happen Phil, are you going to pay us to help you win?'

Phil said, 'Oh, yeah; yeah of course,' or something vague like that. The others weren't convinced by a vague answer like that and one of them asked, 'Well, how much are you going to pay us?' And before Phil could reply, I said: 'I'll give you 100,000 Gilders to share if you help me win.' Well, Phil almost shit himself. He didn't know what to say. He didn't say anything in the end. I wanted to prove something to Phil: it was no good expecting people to work for him just because he was good, he had to pay, they were professionals. I knew I was good for the money – a deal with Peter was a deal.

I was really in form for the race. I remember riding to the start and my calves were so swollen, so full of blood that they were nearly touching the bottle cage on my bike. I'd agreed with Neil that he was going to ride in front of me and I would just fall asleep on his back wheel for 15 of the 20 laps. He'd watch the race, he'd decide what we were going to do in those 15 laps, and all I was going to do was watch his back wheel. Every time a feed came up Neil would drop off and collect my mussette along with his. I would keep riding and he'd catch me up half a lap later and give me my bag, same thing with bottles. I was left to concentrate totally on one thing – the last three or four laps.

At the last feed Neil had to chase with my bag for a lap and a half, and he gave it to me with three to go. By that time a break had been away and the Spanish had brought it back. Then on the back straight I got away with ten riders. It was the break of the day, with Criquielion, Fondriest, Bauer and some others. You can probably remember the finish; it was the one when 'Criq' fell off.

'Criq' attacked on the climb on the last lap, and I remember I was riding on the small ring and 14 or 15 sprocket, so 42 x 14 or 15, and 'Criq' went past on the big ring and 16 sprocket! I thought, this is it. He just motored away on that climb, and then Fondriest went after him. And I saw it on the video later, when Fondriest went past 'Criq' he got a fright. He thought nobody would be able to go with him and next thing he knew, there was Fondriest riding next to him. You could see 'Criq's' head just flick to his right, and his face register, 'Who's this?'

Behind, we were strung out on the climb but we regrouped over the top. Then on the flat it was one attack after the other. Fignon went, I went, Bauer, Gayant, it was a good group. One after the other went, but the group was too strong and we brought everyone back. Eventually Bauer made an attack stick, and it wasn't that he was better than any of us, it was just the luck of the draw. Bauer got lucky. It could have been me, it could have been Fignon, any of us, but it wasn't.

Well you probably know how it turned out, Bauer caught 'Criq' and Fondriest, and in the sprint 'Criq' fell off, Fondriest won and Bauer was disqualified. I attacked with one kilometre to go. I was away but they caught me with about 75 metres to go. It was crushing, absolutely crushing. I could have been on the podium in a World Championship.

I got home that night and I was really upset. Christina gave me a cuddle and said, 'Can't you just be pleased with what you did?' But I couldn't, which is a good thing in one sense. Never being satisfied is what keeps you going in sport, but it creates a lot of frustration for those around you. I realise that now, and actually, when I look back at that ride in the Worlds and think about the ability I had, I did really well. It was a great achievement for a rider of my standard. It was probably the ride of my life.

Also, looking back, what Neil did for me that day was really beautiful, there is no other word to describe it. When I think about how things had been between us only two years before, and he came to Belgium and rode for me like that. He didn't just ride as a domestique, he rode courageously. Without him I couldn't have done what I did. I still can't get my head around how he rode. It wasn't just the money; Neil rode with his heart for me that day, and you don't do anything with your heart just for money, no matter how much it is.

That ride in the Worlds and one I did in the 1988 Tirreno–Adriatico when I was working for Eric Vanderaerden are the two rides in my career I am proudest of. We'd worked as a team all week at Tirreno to help Eric win, and on the last day the race profile said the last 20 kilometres of the stage was flat, but around that area of the Adriatic coast there are no flat roads.

We went through a village with about 20 kilometres to go and we hit this climb, and the bunch just exploded. There were riders everywhere. Lots of little groups forming, and I was with Vanderaerden in the third group. We both got up to the second group, then went down a descent and had to go up another climb. At the bottom, Henk Lubberding, a really good Dutch domestique who had been with Peter Post for ever, gave Vanderaerden a handsling and Eric got on to the back of the front group.

The two other Panasonic domestiques, Guy Nulens and I, were in no man's land, between the groups. I just managed to grit my teeth and get onto Vanderaerden's back wheel, but Nulens got blown out of the back.

Going up this climb the wind was coming from the side, Vanderaerden and I were second last and last man, but to keep Eric out of the wind I moved out into it so he could shelter. Then Eric said to me, 'Go to the front!' So I put my head down again and led him to the front just as we were going over the crest of the climb.

Adriano Baffi had three of his team riding on the front, and Vanderaerden said, 'Ride with them.' I got on the front and now there were four of us going flat out. We went over the top, down;

up another hill, and came to the last kilometre. I led from one kilometre to 600 metres out, and I was breathing through my ears by then. Then one of Baffi's men took over and Baffi sprinted past him, but Vanderaerden just got over Baffi by the line to win the stage.

I coasted in behind them from 600 metres out, but as I crossed the line Giuseppe Saronni was just in front of me, and he turned and nodded his approval at me. Now, I've told you about following Saronni in awe all day in my first Milan–San Remo, so for a guy like him, for one of the greats, to acknowledge with a nod the work I'd just done says more than words could ever do. To do something like that – take hold of a race, put your man in the place to win, prove that your team is the strongest in the race – for me that was more gratifying than anything I won myself.

The role of a domestique is a bit unnatural I suppose. The best domestiques will ride better for someone else than they can do for themselves. You see sometimes on TV in races, there is a time when domestiques will sit up, when things are hopeless or they've just had enough, but the best domestiques never sit up. They ride until they can't ride fast enough any more and riders go past them. I was like that; I never sat up. But your motivation increases ten-fold if you believe in your team leader, and I believed in Vanderaerden. I would have been the same with Phil Anderson. Nulens and I were closest to Vanderaerden and would do anything for him. We never questioned him.

I rode hard for a lot of sprinters in my time, Urs Freuler, Eddy Planckaert and Jean-Paul Van Poppel, but I never rode with my heart for them like I did for Vanderaerden. I think it was because I knew Eric would always be trying to deliver; he was always in there. With Eddy Planckaert, for example, there were always questions. Was he in form? Did he feel like it? Was he too nervous? As a domestique, you can't put yourself on the line for someone you are not 100% certain is doing the same. If you were riding 50 kilometres on the front for Eric, he was going to try in the sprint, whether it meant crashing or not.

Eric was very tough. Earlier in that Tirreno-Adriatico in 1988, he'd crashed, and afterwards, in the showers, his soigneur, Ruud Bakker got a brush and scrubbed all the gravel and dirt out of his wounds. We were staying in this pissy little town, and the only medical thing there was a veterinarian, so Ruud got the vet to sow up Eric's arm. He was a tough guy, a hard bastard.

He was hard in the finishes, too. No one gave Eric any shit. Except one time in the Tour de France when I was riding for Peugeot, Eric and Sean Kelly had such a fight in one finish, they were leaning on each other in the sprint and I think they went over the line with one hanging onto the other's jersey. Neither would give in. They were very alike, Sean and Eric.

Robbie McEwen has that same grit, that same 'I'm going for that wheel and you'd better get out of the way' attitude. Riders are scared of Robbie, not because he's physically big, because he isn't, but because they know he won't give way. He's got that look. You don't see it in every race with Robbie, but when he's on, you know. In the morning there's no point talking to him, because you're not there. He'd walk through you.

It was a good year for me, 1988, my best I think. I did some great work for Panasonic and I did a great ride in the Grand Prix E3–Harelbeke race after Tirreno–Adriatico. I got away with Guido Bontempi, and we were holding off the bunch, but I wouldn't do any work because Eddy Planckaert was in the group behind. Bontempi kept saying, 'Come on we can stay away.' So eventually I said, 'OK, pay me.' He asked me how much I wanted, and I picked a figure out of my head. '200,000 Belgian francs,' I said. And he agreed. So I started working, won a couple of primes that were worth 50,000 Belgian francs each, and we stayed away. Of course Bontempi walloped me in the sprint; he beat me by so much I wasn't even on the same photo with him.

Funny thing – while we were riding Walter Planckaert had driven up alongside me in the team car and asked me what was happening. Why was I working with a better sprinter? I told him, '200,000 Belgian francs,' and he said, 'Oh, OK,' put the brakes on and went back to the bunch.

But I spent the best part of the next year trying to get my money. I would ask Bontempi and he would tell me to ask Boifava, his manager. So I'd ask him and he'd tell me to ask Bontempi. I was swapping backwards and forwards, then at the start of 1989 Post asked me what the score was with the money from Bontempi. I told him they'd been giving me the run-around, so Post went to see Boifava, but he told Post he didn't have it.

That really pissed off Post – a deal was always a deal with him – and he nagged at Boifava for the next four or five months. Eventually they got together one evening in the Giro d'Italia, and Boifava had pieced the money together with bits of currency from all over the place. There were notes from this country and coins from that, but it added up to 200,000 Belgian francs, so Post took it, but he was still angry.

A few days later Zimmerman, who rode for Boifava's team, was away with a Colombian, and they got three minutes lead over a group that contained the race leader, Andy Hampsten. But Hampsten only had one team-mate with him, Ron Keifel, and they couldn't close the gap. Hampsten was losing the Giro.

Then Post put his troops on the front. He had Breukink in second place overall, but is that enough reason to ride? Maybe Hampsten's manager made a deal with Post, and just maybe it was a payback for being messed around by Boifava. They caught Zimmerman with one kilometre to go.

Things like that are happening all the time in cycling, deals being done between riders, manager and teams. On top of that are the sponsor's ambitions and needs, and those of the riders and the directeurs. Then, all this is played out against a backdrop of old scores being settled. It all adds to the fascination, though, don't you think?

20

Cadel Evans

It is the end of April 2005. The last race of the Spring Classics, Liège–Bastogne–Liège is in two days time. I've just got off the phone with Cadel Evans, one of our team leaders at Davitamon-Lotto. We had a good conversation, full of inspiration for Liège and for the coming months, after he placed ninth in the other Ardennes Classic, Flèche–Wallone, on Wednesday.

I had spent some time with Cadel earlier in the week. I picked him up at Brussels airport on Monday and we went to lunch. After that we attended the team medical centre for some tests, and in the evening my wife, Christina, made us dinner. We ate with her and Zane, my son, before going back to my place for the night. Cadel slept in my bed and I slept on the stretcher bed I keep for when Zane stays.

On Tuesday we went out on our bikes, and I took Cadel to ride the Muur in Geraardsbergen, because he'd never seen it before. We met Robbie McEwen and Nick Gates for coffee, before riding home. There, Cadel checked out my books and we talked about his dog, who he loves so much. In the afternoon, Cadel and one of the team masseurs left for their hotel near to the course of Flèche–Wallone. All in all it was good quality time for a directeur to have with a rider.

I wasn't directing the team at Flèche–Wallone; Eric Van Lancker did that job. For the last month Eric and I have been working in Italy and Spain with the team that is going for the hilly Classics. We decided that as Eric, a former winner of Liège–Bastogne–Liège and the Amstel Gold Race, had more experience than me of the hilly Classics, he would direct the team.

I watched the race from home on the television and saw Cadel let two riders pass him on the final ascent of the Mur de Huy, 600 metres from the finish, when he had been in a perfect position. Now he was boxed in, and had to cross to the right of the road before moving forward and getting to the front again. That cost Cadel vital energy, something he couldn't afford to waste on a brutal uphill finish like the Mur.

He hit the front with about 300 metres to go, and as I heard the TV commentator say, 'And Cadel Evans moves to the front,' the hairs on my arms stood up. But Cadel hadn't anything left to capitalise on his position and Danilo Di Luca won, while Cadel fell back to ninth, which wasn't a true reflection of the ride he'd done. He'd made a tactical blunder.

Cadel rang me in the evening to talk, and he was pleased with his ride. We spoke about him letting those two riders pass, and losing position because of that. I told him that it's him or them. You can't afford to be nice, because if you are you lose out. If it means that the other riders fall because you are protecting your position, then so be it. Cadel took my point.

A few weeks before all this, a friend here in Belgium asked me if there were any riders in the team that I got on well with. I told him that it isn't my job to get along with the riders, and it's better to be a little bit distant. But having said that, I can't help feeling a friendship for Robbie McEwen's main domestique, Nick Gates. Nick and I share things on a level that isn't usual in our roles as directeur and rider. He trusts me with personal things in his life, and I do the same with him. And that is not just a 'we are Aussie so we bond' thing, because I have a similar relationship with a young Belgian on our team, Bjorn Leukemans.

In the Tour of the Basque Country two weeks ago I had been confused as to how to handle Cadel Evans; he is different from the average bike rider. I asked Nick's opinion, and he said, 'Get your head out of your arse, Al, and just give him a mouthful of what to do.' I also had dinner with Neil Stephens, who is now an Australian Institute of Sport advisor. Neil has worked with Cadel a lot, and he gave me some more insight into this eccentric young man.

I had first met Cadel in the Tour Down Under in January. We were both making a new start. I was a new team directeur, and Cadel was returning from the cycling scrap heap. After a fantastic career as a champion mountain biker, Cadel crossed over to road racing and lost the Tour of Italy while in the lead, two days from the end. After that he was snapped up by the German squad T-Mobile as back-up to Ullrich, Vinokourov and Kloden, but in his first year with them he broke the same collarbone three times. Last year he won the Tour of Austria, was fourth in the Tour of Lombardy, but was passed over by his team for the Tour de France. Obviously Cadel had brilliant potential, but despite that I hadn't heard one good word about him, not one.

If there is one trait I have that I am proud of, it is always championing the underdog, and as far as I could see Cadel was definitely the underdog. I talked to him and tried to find out what his ambitions were and how he ticked. I concluded that, for a start, it was important that Cadel felt part of the team, but I was afraid that our two Australian domestiques, Gates and Vogels, would be too hard on him as they are both 'tough as nails' characters. But, if anything, they took Cadel under their wing, as a mother bird would with her chicks.

For the team, Cadel is a risk, a shot in the dark. He has a huge amount of potential, but no guarantees. Right from the start, though, the team manger, Marc Sergeant, has given Cadel total support, and now I am personally committed to the challenge of fine tuning this 'rough shod' into a champion. Over the last few months he has slowly consumed me to the point where people say, 'You are always talking about Cadel.' And you know, they're right; he is under my nails.

Lance Armstrong has changed the face of cycling, much like his predecessor Greg Lemond did. Lance has developed a way of preparing for the Tour de France that sees him on the start line each year in perfect physical shape, and with every factor of the course prepared for. In doing that, Lance has beaten a track for anyone to follow. Now, I'm not saying Cadel is a shadow of Lance; that isn't the point I'm making. The point is – what can Cadel do if everything is perfectly in place?

At a recent directeurs' meeting we discussed Cadel's racing programme in the light of his build-up to the Tour de France. We spoke about reconnoitring some of the climbs in the Alps and Pyrenees, and fitting that in with races like the Dauphiné-Libéré and the Tour of Catalonia. We also talked about him riding the

ProTour team time trial in Eindhoven. All I said was, 'If we are going to go for it with Cadel, let's go all the way.' I wanted them to take a chance on Cadel and give him every bit of support we could. If it came to June and he was storming, by then we would have missed the preparation time, and probably he would come up short on his conditioning, which would be a shame.

When I spoke to him on the phone this evening Cadel was bright and excited; he was happy at being so well received by the Belgian fans and by the team. He asked me to make up a list of all the things that I thought could help him in the coming months of build-up to the Tour. Every per cent counts now. In the Basque Country race we spoke of his role and responsibilities as a team leader. More rough edges have to be shaved off before the Tour.

Last night I lay awake thinking about wheel bearings and driving with Cadel to the Alsace area of France to see the route of the stage that goes over the Grand Ballon climb. I am thinking about his time trialling, about replacing the steel bearings in his wheel with ceramic ones, and the position of the gear shift levers on his time trial bike.

The last stage of the Tour of the Basque Country was a time trial on a really technical and very wet course, with a steep one-kilometre hill in it. We worked on getting ready for a time trial, I tried to tell Cadel exactly how to ride; we gave it our best shot. He finished twelfth, and I think he rode too conservatively before the climb. That's another lesson learned.

Before the time trial, Eric Van Lancker got into the team car where I was waiting to follow Cadel with our mechanic and a guest, Neil Stephens. Eric looked at me and said, 'You are nervous.' I admitted that I was, and Eric said, 'Cadel needs to be nervous, not you.' And he was right – to a point. Cadel is under my skin, and I am committed to getting the best Cadel Evans that I can to the start of the Tour de France. I won't be there with him, Hendrick Redant and Herman Frison are our directeurs for the Tour, but he won't need me. If everything is in place, all he'll need is luck.

21

Adri Van der Poel

At the end of 1987 I had signed a contract with Peter Post for two years, but with me having such a good year in 1988, and establishing myself as an integral part of the team, at the end of the season I decided that I had to start cashing in on what I'd done. As a professional sportsman you only have a certain time to make your money, and I realised I had to begin earning what I thought I was worth.

But if you don't ask for more money, you won't get it, so at the end of 1988 I asked Post if we could renegotiate my contract. I still had one year running, but I asked him for a two-year contract, with more in the first year than I was getting under my existing contract, and then a lot more in the second year of the new contract.

We started negotiating, and Peter's first question was, 'Why should I pay you more in the first year when I already have you under contract?' I could see his point, but then my theory was if he paid me more he'd got me for two years. I told him that he'd seen in the last three years that I'd only got better, and that he knew I was giving him everything. I told him he'd got a great team helper, and a rider who was motivated to win races himself if the opportunity came about.

There was a lot of too-ing and fro-ing between me and Post, and eventually the contract was agreed how I wanted it, but when I went into the 1989 season I wasn't up to scratch. I don't know whether it was that or the training I'd been doing over the previous two years, but I didn't feel too good that winter. My blood levels were a bit out of place, especially my cortisol level, which was down on what it had been. I just didn't feel 100 per cent. I also felt that there was a bit of a divide between Peter and myself. Peter Winnen had told me that Post didn't like being dictated to regarding money. He liked to tell you what he thought you were worth, and he didn't like anyone telling him.

I didn't go well in Milan–San Remo. And back in Belgium, at the Grand Prix E3–Harelbeke race, all of a sudden Post suggested that I didn't ride the Three Days of De Panne. He said I should rest up for the Tour of Flanders. Fair enough, but knowing Peter, and that there were always two sides of the coin with him, I was left wondering what the other side was. Considering that in the three previous years I had been seventh, fourth, and second in De Panne I was wondering why he didn't want to take me.

Anyway, I told him that I wanted to ride, so he put me in the team and I finished third overall to Vanderaerden. Eric just beat me in the time trial. Then we came to the Tour of Flanders, and it was really bad weather. Teun Van Vliet and Vanderaerden were our two leaders, but Van Vliet got dropped on the Kwaremont, and Vanderaerden was having a bad day.

I got away in a break early on with Sean Kelly, which didn't succeed, but then I went away again in another break with seven riders, including Marc Sergeant, Dag-Otto Lauritzen and Rolf Sorenson. Later, Edwig Van Hooydonck managed to latch onto us. Then as we came into Geraardsbergen the team car came up next to me. Post was sitting in the passenger-side seat and Walter Planckaert was driving, and Post yelled across, 'Don't ride too much on the front, and stay near Van Hooydonck' – which was fairly logical advice.

We got onto the Muur, and I got over the top with the break. We went down the other side and came to the Bosberg, the last climb. Most of us were climbing on the 42x16 – the Bosberg is quite steep and it was wet that day, so the cobbles were slippery. Suddenly Van Hooydonck attacked from the back of the group in 53x16. There are not many people who could have answered that, and Van Hooydonck took it all the way to the top in the same gear. After the climb we all chased, six of us, but we didn't make any impression on Van Hooydonck. He deserved his victory. He was the best and you couldn't have stopped him winning that day no matter what you had done.

But over the next couple of weeks I felt some animosity in the team. Post didn't even speak to me at Paris–Roubaix, but a few days later at the semi-classic Grand Prix Scheldeprijs he said to me, 'How come you didn't follow my instructions in the Tour of Flanders?' I said, 'What do you mean, didn't follow your instructions?' And he said, 'What did I say in the car?'

Now that was another of his questions that there was no right answer to. So I said, 'You said to me "Don't work too much on the front and stay near Van Hooydonck".' And he said, 'No I didn't, I said to you, not to ride on the front and stay on Van Hooydonck's wheel.' I said, 'Peter, you didn't say that,' but he said, 'Wait here, I'll go and get Walter.'

A few minutes later Post came back with Walter Planckaert, and he asked Walter to tell me exactly what he, Post, had said to me in the Tour of Flanders, and Walter repeated exactly what Post had just said he'd said, agreeing with his version.

I suddenly saw what had happened, I'd got caught up in the Post-Raas rivalry. Van Hooydonck was Raas's rider, and I was taking the flack for him winning. Maybe Raas had said something during the week to Post, rubbing his nose in it maybe, but at the Scheldeprijs it all came to a head.

I was on the outside after that with Post. I heard later that, from then on, he tried never to have me on the team for any big races, so that when I left the team – which was inevitable now – I wouldn't have any FICP points, so I wouldn't have much value. It was a terrible blow, as I still had another year and a half to do with the team. I was gutted, because I knew I could still fly without having shit like that hanging round me.

Looking back now, I wish I'd had the balls to go to Post and tell him that if he didn't want me in the team, then just break the contract. I would have found another team and he wouldn't have had to pay me, but I couldn't do that because I still believed in the team. I was such a team-man. I couldn't understand how I could give so much for the team, how I had ridden with my heart for them, and this was my repayment.

So 1989 sort of flowed on, and I got a few good results at the end of the year, but before that I lost the plot a bit. After my run-in with Post, I couldn't sleep well any more. I would be lying in bed thinking about my situation at night, going over and over it. It got quite bad; my head wouldn't stop working, and sometimes I felt like I was going crazy.

I spoke about my problems to Peter Brotherton in Australia and, Peter being Peter – my guardian angel – he went out and did a course called 'alpha dynamics' and sent me a relaxation tape. It worked, though. From the first moment I listened to that tape it had an effect on me. I started to relax and I started to sleep better. I began to get more focused, and it's a good job I did. Shortly after everything happened with Post I went to the Giro, and in the first week I crashed three times and bust up three bikes. I just wasn't focused any more, I wasn't in my centre. If that happens to you, you are in danger. Luckily the tapes centered me again. I got back in tune with myself, and my intuition began to work again.

That experience sparked off something else, something new in my life. For the first time I started to think about my place in the world, and that there might be more to this existence than just riding a bike. I started questioning everything. You might say that it was my spiritual awakening, but it was a hard awakening because cycling had been everything for me, and being in Panasonic was where I wanted to be. Now, it seemed like the thing I'd wanted most didn't want me.

Still, I got myself together at the end of 1989 and came out in 1990 a stronger person. I was still on the outer with Panasonic – they still didn't want to take me to any big races. I wasn't going to be picked for the Tour or Giro, and they tried not to take me to the Classics. A lot of little things happened, too. Everyone on the team got a mountain bike except me, for example. But somehow, where things like that would have bothered me before, they didn't now. Set against the bigger picture, they just didn't seem to matter any more.

Eventually, Panasonic had to take me to the Giro because they had so many injured riders. Post and Planckaert were both at the Giro, and I'd been leading out Jean-Paul Van Poppel every day, but he was creeping. On one stage I led him out, and with 200 metres to go I was still on the front. I looked behind me and saw a solid wall of sprinters – Van Poppel had lost my wheel. The sprinters swamped me, but afterwards we were in the car and one of the soigneurs said to me, 'Hey, you've got to stop working for Van Poppel. You're fast enough to win here.' And the next day I did it.

I got away with a Frenchman, Pascal Poisson. I don't know how I did it; it just happened because I'd let the race happen without forcing it. It had been splitting and I just hopped from group to group, got to the front, and attacked. The Frenchman got across to me, and we just rode away.

We got into the last 40 kilometres and Poisson's team manager came up – Roger Legeay, my old directeur at Peugeot – and I asked him if I could win. I was prepared to pay, but he just laughed in my face because Poisson was a much faster sprinter than me. Then Walter Planckaert came up and told me not to ride. I asked why, and he said it was because Van Poppel was behind. But I told him that Van Poppel would get dropped on the last climb.

We argued and eventually Walter agreed, but he said, 'You've got to get rid of Poisson on the climb.' Well, the climb was 15 kilometres from the finish – a long way on your own. I attacked a couple of times when we got there, but couldn't drop Poisson, and then he wouldn't work with me any more because I'd attacked him. Eventually, though, he did start riding again.

A few kilometres later Planckaert drove up again and I asked him what had happened to Van Poppel. He told me that he'd been dropped on the climb, so I asked: 'Can I ride now?' And Walter said that I could ride again, but I wasn't to go on the front in the last kilometre.

But coming into the last kilometre we only had six seconds lead on the bunch. Anyway I stayed on Poisson's wheel, but luckily he was so confident he was going to wallop me in the sprint that he kept leading at a good pace, and in the last 200 metres I came off his wheel and just managed to pull past him.

Fred de Bruyne was really happy for me, but at dinner in the hotel that night it was like a funeral. I had given my word to Jose de Cauwer, the directeur of the Tulip Computers team that I would ride for him next year, and Post had found this out. So when he came in he decided to rip strips off me in front of everyone. He was going on about how bad the Tulip team was, how they were all bandits, how I wouldn't get my money. On and on he went, but he didn't bother me any more.

I came out of the Giro riding really well. Steven Rooks and Gert-

Jan Theunisse had joined the team by then, and they had the say about who was going to do the Tour de France. They wanted me to ride, but Post was furious. He told them I was no good, that I would only last ten days, but they said that's all they needed me for. The first ten days – they didn't need me in the mountains. They stood up for me, and Post had to back down.

I went to the Tour, and we won the team time trial, which was the main reason Rooks and Theunisse wanted me there. But over that first week Post wore me down. Every night at the table, snide comments, picking at me. In the end I just packed. Ten days and I packed and went home.

I didn't care any more about what Post was doing, and the team was no longer the focus of my life. Spiritually I think I'd grown, and I was questioning a lot of the things I'd formerly held dear. And I had a contract with Tulip that was worth far in excess of anything I'd had before. So, on every front, it was OK.

Funny thing was, when I was a kid I used to go to church by myself. My mother didn't ever force me, and I didn't go every week, but some Sundays I used to get myself out of bed and go. Religion had always interested me, and now I was reading a lot about it. Even on the Tour in 1990 I had Jehovah's Witness books with me, not that I wanted to become a Jehovah's Witness, I was just interested in religion – in belief, generally.

I still am interested. When I was a kid my mother didn't have me baptized, because she wanted me to make my own mind up about religion and be free to decide whether I accepted the whole concept or not before I did. Now I would like to be baptized, but whenever I have enquired with any religious people about doing it, I found that I have to become something: a Catholic or an Anglican, or whatever. That's not for me. If I become something, then it appears to me that I have to reject the rest, and I can't do that.

I was looking for an explanation to it all. I'd started to wake up to what I was doing. I can remember one day in the Four Days of Dunkirk. I had stopped for a pee and was riding back through the cars, and I looked ahead and saw the bunch winding through the lanes and I thought, what is this all about? This bike race, what does it mean in the scheme of things? I'd never asked those questions before, but it was like I couldn't stop them popping into my head, and I thought maybe religion would have an answer.

Maybe it was because I was tired. Maybe I was just full of cycling – it had been everything to me for a long time. I think now that when I went to Tulip in 1991 it was the beginning of the end of my career. I had had all the trouble with Post, and at the end of 1990 I had split with my wife for the first time. So I went back to Australia. I worked hard there, worked on getting my mindset right. And coming into 1991 I thought I was on top of things again. I had used those confidence-building tapes I have already written about. But when the racing started, and reality set in, I was struggling.

I tried lots of things, lots of techniques and therapies. I began to get in touch with a lot of the anger I'd felt in my youth and tried to resolve that. I came to terms with it, came to terms with a lot of things, but at the same time this searching, questioning, spelt the end of my cycling career.

By resolving those chinks in my personality, by coming to terms with them and removing them, I was losing my drive to succeed. I still trained hard and raced hard, because it was my job. I still wanted to win, wanted to perform and be part of something, but there is a difference between wanting things and needing them. Cycling wasn't essential any more. I started meditating; I was really interested in Eastern religions and meditation. Even on races I was doing it. I can remember sharing rooms with Brian Holm, a Danish rider on the Tulip team, he'd wake up in the morning and see me sat cross-legged on my bed and say in his deep, serious Danish voice, 'Oh Allan, what are you doing?'

But even though it wasn't the be-all and end-all of my life, I was still full of enthusiasm for cycling. I was excited about riding for my new team, and regarded it as a new start for lots of reasons. And I started 1991 quite well.

I rode well in Ruta del Sol. I was in the top twenty in Milan–San Remo, Tour of Flanders and Paris–Roubaix, and I was ninth or tenth in Ghent–Wevelgem. Then we went into May and I crashed in Dunkirk, in the time trial. After that, it seemed like I couldn't pick up the pieces again, and I began to have a problem within the team with Adri Van der Poel. This lasted from then until the following May, and really amounted to bullying in the workplace from Adri.

He was our team leader, and he was a very powerful individual. He had an imposing personality, and none of the other riders would go against him. But Adri always needed a victim, and for some reason, I don't know what it was, he had picked me as his next. Whether it was because I had been riding well at the start of the year and he hadn't been so good, I don't know, but he really made my life miserable. It was worse than with Post, because with Post it was a bit us and them, workers and management, but with Adri I could feel his views being reflected in the attitudes of the other riders around me.

I tried to find the motivation to fight, but it wasn't there like it had been with Panasonic. Van der Poel wasn't riding well. Jonny Dauwe had gone well at the start of the season, and won Kuurne-Brussels-Kuurne, but then he wasn't riding well. There was no all-winning Vanderaerden figure to ride for anymore.

I also struggled with the organisation of the team. Like I have said, with Panasonic everything was perfect. Everything was done to make your life easier, so all you had to do was race. But Jose De Cauwer didn't have Post's attention to detail, although he was a great manager, a great motivator.

The following year, when I really had had enough, before the first race of the year I was sat in my room crying. I had asked myself too many questions and I couldn't see the point of suffering any more. I had had enough of cycling. Jose found me, and I told him that I couldn't get the courage together to ride any more. I said that I'd trained enough, I'd raced enough, I couldn't hurt myself any more and I was frightened of it.

And Jose said, 'I understand, I understand where you are, but why don't you just get your shorts on and go out there today and do whatever you want to do? If you want to ride last man all day, well do that. If you want to ride 20 kilometres and then get off and get in the car, then do it. If you want to attack at the start, do it. Do whatever you want, but don't put any pressure on yourself.' So I raced and I attacked on the first lap and went away with six riders, and the bunch caught me, alone, going into the last lap.

Jose had the ability to talk to someone and allow them to discover in themselves how to achieve something. That is his ability as Belgian National Coach now. His ability has benefited a lot of riders. Greg Lemond had his comeback with De Cauwer, and Eddy Planckaert won the Tour of Flanders with him. He could read what a rider needed, and knew how to support that need.

I don't know why I didn't go and speak to Jose about Van der Poel. I think I was just too unaware in those days, or I lacked the confidence to do it. Why didn't I talk to Post about the shit I had with him? Why didn't I talk to Neil Stephens? Why didn't I talk to Rudy Dhaenens? Why didn't I have the ability to be open and to discuss things? I still don't really have an answer to that one.

But I felt really threatened by Van der Poel. He would do things, like at the end of a stage drive off in a team car, leaving me when there was space in that team car. It got really bad – big things, and little things like my shoes disappearing. And when that happens you start seeing ghosts where there aren't any. I should have confronted him with it, but at that time I didn't know how to. Then, at the start of 1992, all my problems with Van der Poel ended. I don't know why, but it just disappeared.

22

Maurizio Fondriest

It was always going to be my last year. I rode well in the Giro; I was away all day on the Terminillo stage, and Induráin's team chased and caught me on the last climb. I was away on the stage into Bordeaux in the Tour de France, and they caught me with 200 metres to go. And Jose was saying to me, 'Why are you stopping at the end of the year, Allan? You are going well, you can still do it.'

I just felt it was time to stop. After that first race in 1992 where I thought I couldn't race at all, I broke down again in Tirreno–Adriatico. I called Peter Brotherton in Australia, and told him that I was finishing and I was going to take a train home the next day. But Peter said I couldn't finish like that; he told me to try and see it through until the end of the year.

I really shouldn't have been there, though. My spirituality had grown and I was asking too many questions about cycling. The danger with that is what I have already talked about: when you start to question what you are doing, you are not centred any more. To be a pro bike rider you must believe in what you are doing 100 per cent. There is hardly room for anybody or anything else in your life, so there is certainly no room for doubt.

Anyway, I made a deal with God to get me through. I asked Him to look after me and keep me safe until the end of the year, then I would stop. Racing after that became very difficult, and a couple of times I was really frightened. After the stage to Sestrieres in the 1992 Tour de France, which included six cols in 35 degree heat, my heart was racing, and I had bad pains in my chest. I had a really worrying night, and next morning the pain hadn't gone. So I told my soigneur, and he said, 'Oh, don't worry. It's just stress!'

That day there were three cols and a finish on Alpe d'Huez. I suffered badly all day, and when I got to the finish, alone in my hotel room, I laid on my bed and my heart was still pounding. Pounding like I was still in the race, and it didn't slow down for 45 minutes. I was so scared, and I re-made my vow to God that I would stop if I could just get through to the end of the year. After that I picked up, and finished the Tour with a seventh place on the Champs Élysées, but I wasn't going to go back on my vow.

I had an offer from another team, too, from Maurizio Fondriest's team, Lampre. A good offer, but I wouldn't sign. I stuck to the deal I'd made, and Maurizio was really upset with me, although I felt I couldn't tell him why I wouldn't sign. In fact, I haven't ever told anyone why, until now. My heart has worried me for years since, but I had a complete test on it recently, when I got the job offer from Davitamon, and there's absolutely nothing wrong.

I had grown close to Maurizio Fondriest since 1988, and after I retired, no matter what I was doing or how far I was from cycling, he was about the only person from that world I stayed in touch with. I first saw Maurizio race when he was a new pro with Ecoflam-Legnano. He won a stage in Tirreno, and I saw him in a few other races. Then in August 1988 he came to ride the Tour of Belgium, and in those days not many Italians even wanted to race here. He didn't know where he was, and I was riding well – I was third overall that year. I liked Maurizio, from what I'd seen of him, so I made it my business to help him out.

Because it's a small country, the courses in Belgium go this way and that, doubling back on themselves, and it can be very confusing. When I could, I'd tell Maurizio what was coming up on the race route, things like, 'Two kilometres, a sharp right and a cobbled climb' – that sort of thing.

At the finish Maurizio, who it was obvious was going to become a big Italian star, told me that he had a contract to ride the Baracchi Trophy two-man team time trial at the end of the season, and would I like to ride it with him. Of course, I said yes, but two weeks later Fondriest was World Champion and I thought, Well, that's that. There's no way they'll let him ride with me now.' And I just put it out of my head.

Then, a few weeks later, Maurizio's manager called me and asked me if I still wanted to ride the Baracchi with Maurizio. I said yes, and they asked me to go down a week early to train with him, and show him a few things about riding a team time trial because, even though he was World Champion, he was still only a second-year pro.

I stayed with Maurizio, and his mum cooked for us every night. Then, each morning, she would drive us down into the valley to train, because Maurizio lived half-way up a mountain. Once down there we trained behind a derny bike to get some speed into our legs. We had lunch at a hotel in the valley, then a sleep in the early afternoon. Then we trained behind the derny again, this time on our time trial bikes with race wheels in and wearing our skin suits, really simulating the race conditions.

We were both using heart rate monitors, and we could see that our heart rates were about the same for the same riding speed, so we decided to ride at 160 to 165 beats per minute in the race, and see how we went at that. What was interesting was my maximum, or so I thought, was 180 beats per minute, and in the actual race I rode for 60 per cent of the time at 185 beats per minute.

The first year I rode with him, we finished fourth. I remember in the changing rooms after the race, Steven Rooks who had ridden with Gert-Jan Theunisse (they were two of the stars of the Tour de France in 1988) asked me: 'How come you get to ride with the World Champion?' And that sort of spoke to me, spoke to me of how loyal Maurizio was.

And even after I retired, when Maurizio came to Belgium for the Classics he always stayed at my house. I can remember one time when he rode for Panasonic, he had the lend of Peter Post's car and stuck it in my garage. I remember thinking to myself, I bet Peter doesn't know where that is.

Maurizio listened to me a lot, as well: one time he was at my house and he was talking about the pressure he felt he was under in Italy. Everyone was talking to him about what Bugno was doing and what Chiapucci was doing, and I told him not to listen to them, not to worry about what people were saying to him, but just be content with the progress he was making. I was worried that if he'd listened to that pressure, maybe he would have rushed things, and not become the rider he eventually was.

When I went back and trained with Maurizio for the Baracchi in 1989, I was again welcomed into his house like I was one of the family, and everyone wanted to talk to me and welcome me as one of Maurizio's mates. He gave me loads of clothes from his bike shop; the Fondriests and all the people close to them are such generous people.

In 1989 I was due to do three time trials on three consecutive weekends: GP Eddy Merckx; Baracchi Trophy; and the World Cup time trial in Eindhoven. I knew I couldn't peak for all three, so I chose to sacrifice the Eddy Merckx for the other two.

I rode within myself in the GP Eddy Merckx, and next day Post rang me up and off he went again: 'Who do you think you are? You shouldn't be riding the Baracchi. Only the best riders ride the Baracchi. You think you're better than you really are, etc. etc.' They were difficult things for me to hear, but I'd given Maurizio my word and I couldn't back out.

Post wouldn't let me have any special wheels, so I had to borrow some from Maurizio's team, but in the race we started really well. After 60 kilometres we were 45 seconds up on the next team, Laurent Fignon and Thierry Marie. But when Maurizio's manager came up alongside us and told us that, all those words of Post started to flood back into my head. 'Who do you think you are? Only the best riders ride Baracchi. You think you are better than you are.' I kept thinking what Post would say if I cracked, or got dropped, or let Maurizio down.

I saw for the first time what negative energy could do, as I just withered. Maurizio was already having trouble with his back – he had a herniated disc – and he began to slow, too. If I had kept riding like I had been, until those negative thoughts had crept into my head, I think we still could have won it, but in the end we finished second at 45 seconds. We still averaged 51.5 kph over 100 kilometres.

We lost because of my negative thoughts, but I just couldn't block them out. They had been programmed into me. I will never do that to one of my riders now I am in a similar position to Post. I will never give them cause for negative thoughts. If I haven't got something constructive to say, I won't say anything. The crazy thing was that although I was leaving Panasonic to go to Tulip, Maurizio was leaving his team to go to Panasonic, so Post's negativity ended up damaging his own rider.

We still have a bond, Maurizio and I. After I had been retired for a couple of years, he was staying at my house. Christina and I had just bought the place and we were spending quite a lot of money on renovations. We were also building up her business, and that was taking money to do. Maurizio could see all this and asked me how I was off for money, a question only a true friend could ask you. I said I was OK and showed him what I had left and what I had spent, and he said; 'If you ever need any money, you only have to ask.'

That is how Maurizio is: money and material things don't seem so important to him. When you visit his home, he has a car, and his father has a car, and his brother has a car, but they all drive each other's cars. He has a bike shop and a bike brand, and it's Maurizio's money that is invested, and it's his brother, Francesco, who's worked at building the company, but the business doesn't belong to either one of them. Every year at apple harvest time, Maurizio goes to his father's farm to help pick the apples – every year. That really spoke to me about family. It was another awakening. I also felt validated by Maurizio, something else that is very important to me.

Ending my cycling career in 1992 was a relief in a way, although it was pretty heart-rending to let go of something you'd been involved with for so long. But at the same time I felt free, not having to worry about training, about looking after myself so closely, not having to look inwards all the time.

But I also had a big shock waiting for me. In my last couple of years I'd had so many people saying they had work for me when I stopped racing: bike manufacturers, TV companies, magazines, teams who said they wanted me as a directeur or to do PR work. But once I'd retired, nothing came to fruition.

I can remember talking to Stephen Roche a couple of years later during his last Tour de France, and he told me about all the fantastic offers of work he'd had. I told him not to count on them, and a couple of years after that Stephen told me I had been right. A lot of promises are made in cycling, because it gratifies people's egos to make them.

By the time I retired I'd been a racing cyclist for 20 of my 32 years. Bike racing had been my love and my passion for all of my adult life. I made the decision to retire willingly, but I was nowhere near ready for the changes that were about to take place in my life.

* * * * *

I enjoyed the first winter, not worrying about my health, or being obsessed about how my legs felt and always focusing totally on my training. When the new racing season came along in 1993 I did some training camps in Spain with Graham Baxter, and was writing some articles for cycling magazines, but I began to become aware of an emptiness inside me, a void I'd filled, from being a child, with racing. The avenue I had expressed my personality through was gone. I was still Allan Peiper, but I was left without that idea of self that I had created through racing.

I had sold my car back to the garage where I'd bought it, as part of the deal that we made after my Mercedes had been stolen the year before. I was in limbo about the future, and couldn't decide whether I should buy a new car, a good one, when I hadn't anything I could point to as a job yet. So I bought an old Opel, 15 years old it was, with a tick in the motor. That car was a reflection of where I was then – faceless.

How to fill the void? I'd never been to a nightclub, or to a pub. Since I was 12 years old I had been a racer. I'd lived and breathed it, thought of nothing else, so much so that I'd missed out on many aspects of growing up. So I started going out with a mate, getting drunk, really drunk. I got worse: I got a taste for my new life. With a drink inside I had a face, or rather I didn't care if I had one or not. A few times I arrived home at 5 am and fell into bed in a drunken stupor. And then vomited on the floor next to it, while Christina had been awake all night worried about me, waiting for me to get home.

I was only thinking about myself. Professional sports people are like that; they have to be. You, your body, how you feel is crucial to how much you earn – simple as that. But when it's gone, how do you stop thinking of yourself first? I should have stopped being like that, I know, but how do you throw the switch? How do you turn it off, and change? At that point of my life, Allan was first priority, and second. I was also trying to deal with my former life, cycling, not wanting me any more.

My relationship with Christina was being severely tested, but I didn't see it. I was wallowing in hurt and self-pity. I thought I was something, and had run smack into the fact that yes, at one time I might have been, but now I wasn't. I was in a period of transition. That's all it was, but I fucked it up big time. I moved out of our home and went to stay with my fellow Australian, Scott Sunderland, to think for a while.

Christina – my partner for 20 years

Then I had an offer from an organization in England to do a duathlon in Fairford, in Gloucestershire. They would pay my costs and give me some appearance money. They had contracted Steve Ovett as a celebrity runner, and wanted me as the celebrity cyclist. I hadn't wanted to do it at first, but the organizer kept calling, so I agreed. The race was to be held on the first weekend in May, over a distance of 3.5-kilometre run, 40-kilometre bike and finish with a 10-kilometre run. Me against Steve Ovett, but also in with some of the best duathletes in the world.

It was March before I started training a bit more seriously. The running went well and I enjoyed it, but riding my bike was a chore and I couldn't get my head around it. I didn't have to ride my bike – it wasn't my job any more – and suffering on a bike was the last thing I wanted to do for fun. I didn't even have a bike at the time, and had to borrow one to train on. The organizer had arranged for me to ride a Trek bike in the race, as part of a sponsorship deal to cover my appearance money.

Then April arrived – Classics time; my time – and I was a lost soul. I had stopped going out drinking. The duathlon had given me some focus, like a heroin addict being given methadone while he tries to kick the real stuff, but in my heart I was still lost and down. I can remember sitting in the lounge, still dressed in my pyjamas, late one spring afternoon. Ghent–Wevelgem was on the TV, and the overwhelming feeling came over me that where I was wasn't real. Reality was on the TV, and I wasn't part of it any more. At that moment I knew what someone felt like when they were in the state of mind to take their own life. I wasn't there; I wasn't far enough along that feeling – nowhere near it – but I felt something of what it must be like.

In that period there were times when I woke up at night, and went outside and just walked the streets. I know it sounds stupid, but that is how bad my sense of loss felt. My focal point for 20 years had gone and I was in a state of mourning for it, I suppose. It may be that the duathlon saved me. It gave me some focus at a time when my life could have gone completely the other way.

I left for England in my battered old Opel and arrived in Swindon two days before the event. Among the top duathletes taking part was the world champion, Matt Brick from New Zealand, as well as the British and the European champions. Matt was a doctor and a really nice guy, and we clicked straightaway. I got the bike off Trek and set up the position, but I was still less than motivated. There were six of us staying in the organizer's house, and the others were all pumped for the event. But coming from the Tour de France and the pro cycling circuit, this race reminded me of the days back in Australia when I was a youth racing in country towns.

Not that I looked the star. I remember Matt Brick looking at my battered old car, the look of bewilderment on his face asking if this really was the car of a guy who'd been a pro for ten years and won a stage in the Giro and the Tour team time trial. I was embarrassed then, but now I see that time as when I began to re-focus, and began to understand humility and really question the things that society sees as representing success.

Two years ago, one of my friends called me when he found out I was leaving Christina. He told me I was making a big mistake, and that I would regret my decision. I told him that I hadn't asked for his opinion, and that the decision had been tough enough without it. He said we would see in five years whether it was the right decision, whether it had made my life a success or not.

After the Tour of Italy in 2005, when Davitamon-Lotto had won three stages with Robbie McEwen, and we had riders on the front on almost every stage, that friend sent me a text congratulating me on our success. It was a nice gesture, but I wondered if he would have thought that I was a success if I had been living in a camping area, jobless, but nevertheless the happiest man in the world. Society has its own ideas about success, and my old Opel wasn't one of them.

I had no idea what a duathlon would be like, and definitely no idea how to prepare for one. I had been a good prologue rider, but that was different from doing two sports for over an hour at your maximum. The other competitors ate breakfast four hours before the race. I was used to three hours, but I didn't know what the race would ask of my body, or how much fuel I would need, so I ate with them, and a bit less than I normally would.

I had no experience of warming up for a duathlon, and I arrived on the runway at Fairford airfield about ten minutes before the start. It was a cold day, and I stood there freezing. I hadn't put on enough clothes to stand for long, but for the race itself it was too much, and I cooked once we got going.

The first run was hectic, and my pulse hit nearly maximum and stayed there all the way before coming into the changing area in about 35th position. On the bike I started pulling guys in and moved up into third position by the end, but I could feel my strength waning because I hadn't eaten enough, and because I was sweating so much. Inexperience and lack of motivation was catching up on me.

During the last run my legs went to jelly after four kilometres, and I ran on memory after that with a handful of competitors passing me. I was struggling with my head and why in God's name was I subjecting myself to this torture. A television cameraman on a motorbike drew up alongside me and asked me how I felt, to which I said, 'Never again will I do a duathlon.' And I never did.

I finished tenth in the event, which surprised a lot of people, and I knew I could have done much better with the right preparation and attitude, but at that time in my life I had done all that. I'd been all I could be in a sport. Still, the Fairford duathlon had given me a focus, and brought some sanity into my life. Not long after it I moved back home. The transition was beginning to pass, and a new era about to dawn, the one where I'd put my partner first and begin a search for the true Allan Peiper, although it was still to be a bumpy ride.

I carried on doing some bike tests for magazines, and I enjoyed doing that and writing about the bikes. I didn't want to write articles about my own experiences, though. I didn't want to keep re-hashing the same old stuff. I wanted to do something creative. I did a bit of TV on the back of the motorcycle for Channel 4, some stuff on the Giro and Tour for SBS in Australia, and for ESPN in America. I enjoyed the TV work: I had to make my own little programmes, and it was really interesting. But all these things didn't add up to one big thing, to one job where you could say, 'I'm Allan Peiper and I'm a TV reporter, or I'm a journalist.' I needed that to hold on to. I've always needed a place, an identity.

Finally, I went to do a training camp in Palo Alto in California, and I had a bit of a crisis. I just couldn't speak any more about cycling. I felt I had no enthusiasm and yet I was taking the money, which was wrong. All the people buying magazines and going to training camps were doing so because of their passion for cycling, and all they got was some burned-out old pro raking over his past. So I stopped. I stopped everything connected with cycling. I wrote to the magazines to tell them of my decision, and I even asked them to stop sending me free copies. I found out later that some of them thought I'd had a breakdown.

Soon after I stopped racing I had discovered a method of meditation called Kriya Yoga. I read a couple of books on it and found a space at home where I could do it. I took up a course of Shiatsu pressure-point massage, and did that for a year. I had between five and ten people coming for a massage each week. Some pro riders came in as well.

That was ticking over nicely, and maybe would have grown into a practice, but I needed it to be an instant success, and be accepted again. I needed people to say it was the best Shiatsu massage they'd ever had, and I needed them to rush enthusiastically around their mates telling them to go and see Peiper – he's brilliant. I was barking up the same tree again, the tree of needing acceptance and approval I'd just walked away from.

I was lurching around in the dark really, and finally I realised I had to completely turn my back on cycling. I needed to make a new start in a completely different world. Anything to do with cycling at that time of life and I was going to drag a whole lot of shit behind me while I was doing it.

My wife had a fast-food business, and one day she said, 'Look, why don't you come in with me and we can earn a good dollar and you'll have a great life?' So I did. She had supported me during my career, and it was my turn to help her with hers. It was good for me: we restored the house we'd bought; we worked hard together; and I got some semblance of order into my life.

I kept on with my spiritual search, too. I meditated. I went to India twice. I spent some time in an Ashram in the Himalayas on one trip, getting up at four o'clock in the morning and washing in a freezing cold mountain stream. Singing and meditating, and being confronted with my attachment to the western world, I realised how safe I was in my little house.

It was a great time of discovery for me. I never quite lost sight of cycling, but we were on different paths. It was a very valuable time. I saw and experienced many things that were impossible to do as a cyclist. And I began to learn about humility, although that took a lot of time.

After a couple of years a chance came to do some TV work on the Prudential Tour in the UK. It was a very good offer, but I turned it down. I wasn't ready to go. I'd had a lot of negative comment about selling hamburgers for a living. 'Hero to zero. Look at him now, he used to be a pro bike rider and now he's selling hamburgers'. That sort of thing. And I didn't want to put myself in the firing line for more of that. I didn't want to be in England on the TV, signing autographs, then come back to Belgium to be laughed at again. It was self-preservation.

But through selling hamburgers I eventually found humbleness and humility. I understood the lives people led, people I'd only flashed past on the road before, and the struggles they had to pay the bills and feed their families. Being responsible for paying people's wages, too, was a new and big responsibility. It was a good learning process, and a good grounding for the place I'm at in my life now.

And you have to endure the bad times in order to appreciate the good. I remember going to work selling hamburgers one Wednesday at a fair, and all I took was £20. I got a parking fine that cost me £25, and I bought a Valentine's Day cake for my wife that cost another £10. So I was £15 down for the day.

My life, like everyone's, has been a roller-coaster ride. And writing this has helped me realise that some of the troughs as well as the peaks have been my own doing. My early life created a lot of problems for me, and they still crop up now and again, but I try and catch myself when they do. But now, for the first time in a long time, I feel I'm in the right place at the right time.

I've come to terms with my cycling career. I've come to terms with my spirituality. Going to India taught me that I am western, not Indian. I looked for answers in the beliefs of others, but now I have my own beliefs. I believe there is a God, but I can't believe in one group's God. And I love cycling. It's in my heart, and I hope I can do some good now that I'm back in it.

For a lot of years I've moaned about the weather in Belgium – part of my obsession with the little things that are wrong. Recently I've stopped doing that. Come to think of it, I never did it when I was racing, either. Quite the contrary, I used to wake in the morning and if the rain was drumming on the windows I'd think: good, my rivals won't be out today and I'll have one over them. I am focused again, Allan Peiper is back. Without all the spiky edges and hang-ups this time, I hope.

23

Allan Peiper – 2005

It is 5 July 2005, and today was stage four of the Tour de France. Lance Armstrong pulled the Yellow Jersey over his shoulders for the first time in this year's Tour, after he and his Discovery Channel team won the team time trial from Tours to Blois.

My Davitamon-Lotto team finished a respectable 11th, and I would have loved to have been with the boys, but we have four directeurs sportifs and only the two most experienced can go, so Hendrick Redant and Herman Frison are on the Tour while I have to watch on TV.

When I was racing, if I wasn't in it I wanted the Tour to be over as quickly as possible. It's like you are an accessory to the team, not part of it. Now that I'm a directeur I have the same feeling, but I understand that the most experienced have to go because I saw how demanding a grand tour can be when I was directeur at the Tour of Italy this year, and the Giro is no comparison with the Tour.

I rang Herman Frison after stage three of the Tour de France, where our sprinter Robbie McEwen was disqualified for using his head while duelling with Stuart O'Grady in the sprint. Herman did the Giro with me, and now he was in the first car in the Tour. He told me how much harder the Tour was for a directeur than the Giro, and I had the feeling he felt a little bit out of his depth, but he will find his way; he has no choice. The call cheered me up. After it, I knew I wasn't ready for the Tour yet.

The Tour of Italy was an adventure for both Herman and myself. Herman had done the Tour of Spain last year, but now he was leading a big team with riders who could play a part in a ProTour race. We had McEwen and Tom Steels for the sprints, and lead-out men for them in Nick Gates, Henk Vogels and Bjorn Leukemans. Then we had Mauricio Ardila, Wim Van Huffel and Christophe Brandt for the mountains. A good team, but we had some problems in the run-up to the Giro. McEwen had been ill during the spring, and although he won a stage in his comeback race in Germany, to win against Petacchi in the Giro would be a different kettle of fish. Steels had also been sick and had been beaten by Petacchi in stage one in the Tour of Romandie two weeks before.

At the start of this year I was inspired by the role I could play in this team, but when I look back I have to admit that naïve would be a good description of how I was. I was so positive about what I could do, the difference I could make, but I didn't have the experience of dealing with the different personalities that make up a team when they are in a stress situation. The Giro this year gave me a quick, three-week lesson.

Arriving at the boot of Italy in Reggio Calabria for the start we were designated a hotel six kilometres up a mountain, and 40 kilometres from the prologue course. It was to be a short prologue of only 1,150 metres, the second-shortest ever, on a straight strip of road along the beach front at night. Speed was what the riders needed, and there we were on top of a mountain. Training on climbs wasn't what was on order, so for the three days before the race we spent the time descending and ascending the mountain in cars with the bikes on the roof to train on the flat – in between meetings and bad weather.

Belgian Champion Tom Steels was one of the favourites for the prologue, but already ill before the start he under-performed and retired on stage two with a bladder and kidney infection. First problem. Robbie McEwen went better and was 15th in the prologue, but as the night wore on and during the repeated following of riders along the floodlit strip of road, I had a phone call from the doping control doctor. One of our riders had been told just before he started that he was needed to go to the control to give a sample, and he hadn't turned up. Big problem.

What happened was, during the 1,150 metres he forgot! And had left for the hotel in a team car. He had ten minutes to get back to the control at the finish and give his sample, otherwise it was all over. He would be deemed positive, and his contract terminated. I left Frison to do the driving, phoned the team car and told them to turn around and get back immediately while I rode to the control on a bike. The rider in question arrived back, and we got it sorted out. All of this was before the race, proper, had even started.

Robbie was beaten on stage one by an unleashed Bettini, the one we hadn't seen all season, who attacked at the base of the climb to the finish and no one could follow. After the finish Leukemans was called to the doping control. I went to the trailer with him and he gave the required 150 ml of urine, but the doctor wanted some more. Bjorn had no urine left, so he drank two litres of water to get his system going. It took two hours to get 20 ml more. We then had to drive 125 kilometres back to the hotel, arriving at 9 pm. Leukemans then had to eat and get ready for tomorrow. For a rider, things like that take away recovery time; for the directeur it's more mentally tiring.

Stage two saw a group get away early and take an eight-minute lead. Fassa Bortolo, Petacchi's team, asked us to put three of our riders on the front to work with them to bring the group back so McEwen and Petacchi could sprint it out at the end. Herman and I decided to go along with it, so Herman told the riders over the radio to ride with Fassa, but our boys didn't want to do it. Dilemma.

Fassa brought the gap down to three minutes, then with 50 kilometres to go Nick Gates took over for our team. The race had just gone live on TV, and Nick did the bulk of the work for the next 40 kilometres. Then Robbie won the stage. It was a great start, even though I then had to go with Robbie to the control where he had the same problem as Leukemans, and I had to sit there waiting until his waterworks got into action again. Good job a directeur sportif – you spend a lot of time waiting for someone to piss.

Davitamon-Lotto rode a superb Giro, both as a team and as individuals. We won the super team competition for the most consistent team in a points-based competition, and the team bonded from the moment of that first stage win of Robbie's. The win bonded them, but they also bonded because of Nick Gates. Nick had ridden 45 kilometres on the front in TV time and the world was impressed. He grew in stature as the comments came in, and the other riders felt the power of success as a team. The ball had started rolling.

Next day a group got away, and Herman asked over the radio which team was chasing. 'We are,' said one of our riders, a stark contrast to the day before. We had told the riders at a meeting in the morning that we made the decisions, not them. They could discuss, but in the end we decided tactics. Now they had taken the responsibility.

In the next days and weeks, Ardila finished third and Leukemans fourth behind Danilo Di Luca in an uphill sprint. Christophe Brandt was second after a long breakaway. Van Huffel was the revelation of the Giro, climbing with the best, ending in the top ten on three mountain stages and 11th on general classification. Mauricio Ardila had, in his efforts to help Van Huffel's rise in the overall, single-handedly brought the Discovery Channel rider, Paolo Savoldelli, back from losing the Pink Jersey to Gilberto Simoni on the penultimate stage. A Belgian team had left its stamp on the Giro d'Italia.

Victory is not for everybody, and sentiment was divided in the team when Henk Vogels took off with 1,500 metres to go on a stage after Robbie had left a gap for him going into a corner. Henk rode for the biggest win of his career at 60 kph, until he was swamped just before the line. Robbie won, Henk was fifth. We didn't know whether to be happy or sad.

After that stage I received a text from our team manager, Marc Sergeant, congratulating the team and me personally for doing a great job, and confirming the faith he had in me when he gave me my job. I sent a text back saying thanks, but I said the most important thing was to keep my feet on the ground because success can change in an instant.

I had hardly finished sending that message when I received a call from our hotel to say that our doctor had been taken into custody by the Italian police for possessing an altitude trainer, a machine he uses to aid our rider's recovery. Only one country, Italy, has outlawed these machines, and a technicality in the wording of the law allowed the police to take the doctor for questioning. I was speechless. McEwen wins his second stage; Vogels comes so close in a brave attempt, and that creates euphoria in the team. Then you get news that a friend and colleague has been locked up by the police. Talk about a mess of emotions.

There was a mass of reporters and TV cameras waiting at the hotel for our arrival, but we had orders not to talk to them because a press release was being prepared. On a more practical side, we didn't know where the doctor was and didn't know when he'd be back, so the riders had no recovery aid, and one of them had a fever and another a bad cold. On top of that, all his medications had been confiscated, and we still had two weeks left to race. We were looking down the barrel of a gun, but things were about to get worse.

The Saunier Duval team was in the same hotel as us, and when our doctor was arrested theirs panicked and threw all their allowed substances out of her bedroom window. Unfortunately the police, stationed downstairs, saw all this and called in the drugs squad.

In the last decade the authorities have done their best to stamp out drugs in cycling. But it's been like drugs in society: close down one avenue and another opens. The police know this, plus when they'd done raids before they had found drugs, so although our doctor was released at midnight, all his medications and those of Saunier Duval were confiscated. The medications had all been sanctioned by the UCI, but a new law had been passed in Italy which said that no intravenous injections could be given to a rider unless he was sick, and then only at a hospital. That was the basis for the confiscation.

It's tiring, mentally and physically, being a directeur. Long days, little rest and constantly looking after other people and their problems, while having your own shit to deal with as well. It's hard to find a functioning balance. On top of that, I am an emotional person and can cry at the slightest hint of joy or grief. That awareness makes things even more complicated in a job where you have to come last in the list of your priorities of who or what needs looking after.

Robbie took his third stage win the day after the first rest day. In an epic sprint between some of the giants of the game, Robbie beat Petacchi and Zabel by a tyre's width. It was a pure win – no ifs or buts – with Robbie getting the better of the fastest man in the world. When I stood in front of the podium as Robbie received the winner's flowers and points jersey, waiting to take him to the dope control, I had the feeling that this was child's play – our team was dominating.

It was a good feeling to be part of that success and play my role in it. At moments like that all the things that get in the way every day, and need to be organized and sorted out for the team behind the scenes, fade away, and are of no importance any more. Success makes it all worthwhile, and I was filled with pride.

Then I received a text message. Cadel Evans had crashed on a descent while doing reconnaissance of one of the Tour de France stages, and had broken his collar bone. Take that uppercut while your guard is down. How can that happen, and now of all times, amid such success? Cadel's Tour looked to be over. All his dreams; all the work and support that had gone into making his Tour debut perfect, after years of being sidelined by broken bones and not fitting into the T-Mobile team; all I had given of myself to that challenge. All gone. I was gutted for Cadel.

But this was Robbie's day, though, his third win and what a win! The team had been super all day and my work that night had to be for them, I would call Cadel later. Doping control, drive to the hotel, check the personnel are OK, make up the programme for the next day, map and race book checking, writing reports for the bosses back in Belgium. It was 9.30 when I stepped into the shower, tired, stressed, hungry and emotional, but I was alone for the first time since seven that morning. The moment the water hit me, the tears came, and that ten minute shower was the length of time I cried. Fuck, I'm not ashamed of it. I am proud, because it means I care. I care enough for it to hurt, and I'm proud that I feel responsible for my riders, that they aren't just numbers or disposable items. The day I become numb, and don't care, is the day I need to be looking for another job. But then maybe the job I've got would be easier if I didn't care so much.

I followed Axel Merckx in the team car during his epic stage win at the Dauphiné Libéré in June 2005. He was alone for the last 100 kilometres of a mountain stage, and I was right behind him when he threw his arms in the air on crossing the finish line. I had seen him attack and witnessed the gallant suffering as he fought to hold onto his lead. After the line he was mobbed by a hoard of reporters, but I drove on to where our bus was parked, I could congratulate him later. I'm like that: I refuse to run after the winner. What I want to do is be there for the rider who is struggling with his form, his life or with his mind. He needs my support in the hard times, because in cycling there are more of those than success. Anyway, when they're successful they don't need your help.

The Tour of Italy was a test for me, a test of my concentration and ability to lead, and still be able to listen. It was difficult, because I've always taken things personally, but during the Giro, with everyone fatigued and stressed out, I realised that the only way to get by is to let it all roll over you.

But keeping your emotions in balance while performing the juggling act of keeping 20 people living on top of each other happy on a day to day basis, while organizing and planning, as well as listening and understanding, challenged my willpower time after time. At best, behind the success of the team, my first Grand Tour was like nearly drowning, then coming up for air, only to go down again.

It's been like that all year really. Learning to cope with new things, new responsibilities, experiences and expectations. Things have moved on, and as I write the last passage of this book, I've just come back from a hectic Tour of Germany, my first ProTour race on my own as a directeur. But the good news is I'm still swimming, and not drowning; at least, I don't think I am.

The German tour was a week of tension with two inexperienced personnel to work with, and no second directeur. We have a team doing the Tour of Spain with two directeurs, and then there were races in Belgium that needed another. There was no choice; the buck stopped (and started) with me.

The race began on a Monday, with me in one team car and the doctor driving the other, and on the first day the camper van broke down; it just limped to the finish. We need the van for carrying the riders in some sort of comfort to and from hotels, but luckily I arranged with Sean Yates for my riders to go to the hotel in the Discovery bus, while I drove behind the camper in case it stopped completely.

We stopped at a garage, and they pulled out all the stops to fix the camper van, but that was only the start of my mechanical troubles. Second day the equipment truck radiator burst; third day the washing machine gave out; fourth day the team car catalyser blew 500 metres from a mountain top finish – at 2,700 metres altitude!

I got a driver from Belgium to bring a new team car during the night, ready for the next stage and, as I write this, my car is still in

Austria waiting for new parts. Oh, and my television in the team car, and the radios I talk to the riders with, all gave out.

Before the Tour of Germany I heard from Hendrick Redant that the race organiser had told him that on the Solden Glacier stage the riders would need a 27 sprocket, the climb was so severe. I told the head mechanic to get some for us, but the powers above me decided that we would get by with 25s.

It was the crucial stage, and as I passed my riders one by one on the climb I could see that they were all over-geared. Wim Van Huffel has revealed himself as a great climber this year, but he was pulling on his handlebars, all over his bike, in a desperate effort to keep up. Van Huffel normally climbs in the saddle, but because of the gear he was out of it, pulling with his skinny arms. It wasn't a pretty sight.

Most of the other riders had a 27 or 28 sprocket and the leader of the ProTour, Danilo Di Luca, had a 29. At the front, Jorg Jaksche from Libert Seguros was zig-zagging across the road and got dropped, so that left four. Jan Ullrich from T-Mobile, Levi Leipheimer and Georg Tötschnig from Gerolsteiner, and my boy from Davitamon-Lotto, Cadel Evans. The other three were sitting down pedalling, as should Cadel have been, but he couldn't get on top of his gear. Leipheimer was doing it easily and must have had a 28 sprocket.

All of a sudden Ullrich cracked and went off. Evans was still there, but Leipheimer increased the pace and the two Gerolsteiner riders went away. It was frustrating to watch, knowing your rider was hampered by the lack of something as simple as one sprocket. Ullrich was 100 metres behind Cadel, but got two running pushes from supporters right up to and past Cadel, and by that time the German had found his legs again.

Ullrich got another push, and he went away and took 20 seconds from Cadel by the finish. Over-geared and disadvantaged by the help Ullrich had received, Cadel came in fourth. To be a directeur you have to be constantly swapping hats. One minute you are an advisor, then an organizer, then a psychologist.

When the team car blew 500 metres from the top of a climb, my first priority had to be getting the riders down to our hotel. I had to leave it there, stranded, and get them down in the one remaining car we had. That done, it was time to organise insurance, a tow truck and a spare team car for next morning. I got to bed that night thinking, 'I can't do this job; it's too much for me.'

But the next morning you get up and do it all again. Being alone in Germany was difficult, but the managers must have had faith in me to think I could pull it off. Since the start of the year I have had to learn so many aspects of a job that is so intricate and ever changing, taking control of the team alone was just the culmination of all I've learned.

Three days after the mechanical problems, and after a long, wet trek for the riders through the Black Forest, Cadel Evans triumphed in a stage that finished on top of the Feldberg. As I heard his name on the radio, which was working fine now, the feeling of relief and joy after the frustrations of the previous days overwhelmed me. The behind-the-scenes fiascoes that had repeated themselves, day after day, through breakdowns and disputes among the support crew, had now found their counter polarity.

I find it hard to place all those things. To balance the stress and frustration of running a team with the joy of success, while trying to stay balanced and focused enough to see and feel what is really happening, is not an easy task when you are being tested on all fronts.

Directly after Cadel's stage-win I had to take the driver, who had brought the spare team car from Belgium, to Zurich airport, and then drive 450 kilometres to the team's hotel in Luwigshaven, back in Germany. The champagne had been drunk, but they'd saved a glass for me, although there was no food. I was beside myself with hunger and fatigue, but the schedule for next day's time trial still needed finishing so everybody would know what they were doing. I had worked it out roughly the night before, but exact times of departure from the hotel to the start, and who would be following whom in what vehicle, still needed filling in.

By chance, I passed Cadel in the lobby. 'Good job, today,' he said, and reminded me about the gloves I'd sent with another rider to give him at the front, and about the dark chocolate wrapped in silver paper someone took him later. Things like that are fantastic for morale on a bleak, cold and rainy day. A word of praise like that, Cadel remembering and thanking for those things, makes all the other aspects of my job seem worthwhile.

There had been rumours for a couple of months that one of the four directeurs in our team would have to go next year. I figured that with the least experience of the four, and being Australian, that it would be my head on the chopping block. I can't say that the thought didn't disturb me, but there was nothing I could do about it if it was me to go. I would just have to move on and find another job, and another place in life. I knew that I had some support; one of our riders, the double Tour of Flanders winner, Peter Van Petegem, said that during the Tour de France he and Robbie McEwen had talked about the rumour, and they were both behind me staying. As it turns out now I wasn't in line for the sack, but until the papers are signed nothing is for certain.

I had a call from our manager, Marc Sergeant, last week. He said he was surprised that I was worried about my position. In a team that has had so much success this year, you would think everybody was safe, but the problem is that the world of cycling is an ever changing one, and for the support team of directeurs, doctors, masseurs and mechanics one year of security at a time is very often about all you can hope for.

I have a meeting today with our manager, and I think it is to talk about next year. I have made so much progress this year, having had to learn everything from day one. The feeling crossed my mind the other day that I was actually good at this job, and would be really good at it in a couple of years. I also found out that Robbie had told our sponsor, Marc Couke from Davitamon, the same thing. If the riders have faith in me and I do my best, which is all I can ask of myself, then I have a place in cycling. It really is a dream job, believe me, despite the problems – being among the best riders in the world, seeing them win, picking them up after they don't, or after they fall. It's the next best thing to racing yourself.

Allan Peiper's Palmarés

1977 (Junior)
3rd World Championship
points competition (track)

1978 (Junior)
2nd World Championship
points competition (track)

1981
1st Dulux Tour (New Zealand)

(Allan's early career as a junior
and amateur was so prolific, we
haven't the space for all his wins.
He won many major events as
well of dozens as smaller races
in Australia and Europe,
especially in Belgium.)

1983 (Peugeot)
1st Harrogate*
1st Thirsk*
2nd Meulebeke*
2nd Manchester*
2nd Ninove (1)*
3rd Ninove (2)*
4th US Pro Championships
6th Tour of America

1984 (Peugeot)
1st Tour of Sweden
    1st stage 8
1st Tour de l'Oise
    1st Prologue
l'Etoile de Bessèges
    1st Prologue

Critérium du Dauphiné
    1st Prologue
95th Tour de France
    3rd Prologue
    3rd stage 1
3rd Maarheeze*

1985 (Peugeot)
Paris–Nice
    1st Prologue
Tour de l'Oise
    1st Prologue
3rd Grand Prix de Cannes
24th Tour of Flanders
86th Tour de France

1986 (Panasonic)
1st Grand Prix Impanis
Tour of Belgium
    1st Stage 4
2nd Sun Tour
    1st Stage 3
    1st Stage 9
    1st Stage 15
1st Birmingham*
1st Zwevezele*
1st Brisbane*
Tour of Spain
    2nd Prologue
3rd Championship of Flanders
5th Tour of Denmark
8th Three Days of La Panne
116th Giro d'Italia

1987 (Panasonic)
1st Grand Prix d'Isbergues

177

Tour of Britain
    1st Stage 1
1st Templeuve*
2nd Bavikhove*
2nd Cork *Eire)*
4th Three Days of La Panne
5th Ghent–Wevelgem
10 Tour of Flanders

1988 (Panasonic)
Nissan Tour of Ireland
    1st Stage 5
    11th Overall
Sun Tour
    1st Stage 1
    1st Stage 10
    4th Overall
1st Geraardsbergen*
2nd Three Days of La Panne
2nd Woerden*
3rd Tour of Belgium
4th Tour of Denmark
4th Trophy Barrachi
    (with M. Fondriest)
5th Four Days of Dunkerque
6th Tour of Mediterranean
10th World Road Champion-
ship
10th Championship of Zurich
103rd Giro d'Italia

1989 (Panasonic-Isostar)
2nd Trophy Barrachi
    (with M. Fondriest)
3rd Three Days of La Panne

4th Tour of Denmark
4th Tour of Belgium
7th Tour of Flanders

1990 (Panasonic-Sportlife)
Giro d'Italia
    1st Stage 14
1st Wetteren*
4th Tour de Vendée
6th Tour of Belgium
11th Tour of Holland
8th Four Days of Dunkerque
16th Paris–Brusselles
144th Giro d'Italia

1991 (Tulip Computers)
1st Malderen*
4th New Jersey Citibank GP
    (USA)
6th Tour of Britain
10th Tour of Holland
10th Ghent–Wevelgem
16th Tour of Flanders
22nd Paris–Roubaix
49th World Road Champion-
ship

1992 (Tulip Computers)
126th Tour de France
130th Giro d'Italia

* Criterium/Kermesse

178